Daoism Explained

IDEAS EXPLAINED™

Hans-Georg Moeller, *Daoism Explained*

Joan Weiner, *Frege Explained*

Daoism Explained

From the Dream
of the Butterfly to the
Fishnet Allegory

HANS-GEORG MOELLER

OPEN COURT
Chicago and La Salle, Illinois

Volume 1 in the Ideas Explained™ Series

Cover image: *Festival of the Peaches of Longevity (P'an-t'ao t'u)*, 14th-15th century Ming Dynasty (1368–1644). Handscroll, ink, color, gold on silk. The Nelson-Atkins Museum of Art, Kansas City, Missouri (Gift of the Herman R. and Helen Sutherland Foundation Fund) F72-39. Photography by Robert Newcombe. Reproduced with permission.

To order books from Open Court, call toll-free 1-800-815-2280, or visit our website at www.opencourtbooks.com.

Originally published in German as *In der Mitte des Kreises: Daoistisches Denken* (Insel Verlag, 2001).

Open Court Publishing Company is a division of Carus Publishing Company.

First printing 2004
Second printing 2005

Printed and bound in the United States of America.

Library of Congress Cataloging-in-Publication Data

Moeller, Hans-Georg, 1964-
    Daoism explained : from the dream of the butterfly to the fishnet allegory / Hans-Georg Moeller.
        p.   cm.
    Includes bibliographical references and index.
    ISBN 0-8126-9563-1 (pbk. : alk. paper)
    1. Philosophy, Taoist.   I. Title.
 B162.7.M63 2004
 181'.114—dc22

                                                                    2004012884

Contents

Preface

The understanding of Daoist philosophy has made impressive progress in the past two or three decades. Important excavations in the 1970s and 1990s have greatly increased our knowledge of its formative stages. Much improved translations of the great Daoist classics (such as those of the *Laozi* by Roger T. Ames and David Hall, by Robert G. Henricks, and by Philip J. Ivanhoe[1]) have been published, and in addition to this, many texts that remained entirely inaccessible to Western readers have been recently made available in English, French, or German.

This advancement in scholarship has brought about a new perception of Daoist thought—it is no longer explained mainly in terms of the metaphysical tradition of the West, but more and more recognized as a philosophy that has something unique to offer. Earlier "Western" prejudices about Daoism have been removed: the Dao is now rarely described in the "Godlike" fashion of an absolute origin or ultimate principle, but rather as the smooth way of nature, as the ongoing process of fertility and production, of living and dying. Similarly, there is now practically unanimous agreement that the Daoist strategy of nonaction (*wu wei*) is not merely some fundamental passivity which corresponds to a principle of "nonbeing," but rather a paradoxical way of allowing the most effective and perfect action to occur.

Still, I believe, the process of unearthing Daoist philosophy out of the metaphysical ballast from which it had been covered by earlier "Westernizations" (not only by Western interpreters) is not yet complete. It is, for instance, still often held that the Dao is some profound idea that is almost beyond comprehension, or that it is something so mystical that it renders all language futile. But if the Dao is not a transcendent principle, if it is not *beyond*, but rather natural and simple and this-worldly—why should it be such a complicated idea, why should it be an *idea* at all? Moreover, if the strategy of nonaction does not imply total passivity, why should it be different with language—especially given the fact that the Daoists so often insisted on the parallel function of action and language?

This book is meant to further loosen the metaphysical interpretation of Daoist philosophy. Daoist philosophers were in many ways different from their ancient and modern Western counterparts. They were not so much concerned with profound thoughts and deep meanings—they were rather experts in how to avoid these philosophical pitfalls. And they did not aim at transcending the limits of time and space or of language and thought, but were much more willing to cultivate an attitude that allowed for a perfect affirmation and appreciation of all that lives and dies, of all that is said and thought.

I begin this journey through Daoist philosophy (after a short historical overview) by taking a close look at the imagery it invented. It is precisely through its images and allegories—specifically in the two masterpieces *Laozi* and *Zhuangzi*—that Daoism fascinates, and I don't think that one can really understand Daoist philosophy without understanding the verses about the valley and the root, or the stories about the butterfly and the fishnet. In part I, the images analyzed provide access to the great topics of Daoist philosophy discussed in part II, most important of which is probably the perennial issue of life and death. In part III, I describe the philosophical structure or architecture which shapes the Daoist worldview; and, finally, in part IV, I attempt to point out how Daoist philosophy relates to other philosophical trends, with a special focus on what it may contribute to the philosophy of our time.

I am very grateful to Shaw Moi for reading the manuscript and to Ryan O'Neill and Cindy Pineo for making my English more English—or, at least, more Canadian.

Cedar Bay, June 2004

INTRODUCTION

A Very Short History of Daoism

Laozi and the *Daodejing*

The history of Daoism began, as we now assume, with a text that is today known under the title of the *Laozi* (*Lao Tzu*) or the *Daodejing* (*Tao Te Ching*). This is a rather short book consisting of eighty-one philosophical and poetical sayings. If one holds an English (or French or Spanish or German) translation of it in one's hands today, it is most likely based on an edition of the *Laozi* that dates back to a Chinese philosopher named Wang Bi who lived in the third century CE. When Wang Bi was still in his late teens or early twenties (he died at the age of twenty-three), he thoroughly studied the *Daodejing*. He added concise comments to the lines and verses of the text to explain its philosophical meaning. Later on, perhaps because of its philosophical insightfulness, Wang Bi's edition of the *Daodejing* became the "standard version": While many other ancient editions and commentaries were partly or completely lost, Wang Bi's version was often copied or printed, and his interpretation of the text became the most prominent and influential one. Thus, the book of *Laozi*—now for many decades a "classic" not only in China but also on a global scale—is generally known in a form it took on in the third century.

It had, however, always been clear that the "original" *Laozi* was much older and, of course, not written by either Wang Bi or any other of its early Chinese editors. What was entirely unclear, though, was exactly how old it was and who specifically had been its author. The question of the age and the authorship of the *Daodejing* has been a riddle for centuries. However, now it appears

1

that this question is not only unsolvable, but wrongly asked. In fact, it seems that the *Daodejing* never had an author in the strict sense of the word and was not even written at a specific time.

Many ancient Chinese historical and philosophical sources from the first and second century BCE mention the *Laozi*, but none of these early versions of the text had been preserved or transmitted into modern times. (The ancient writings also frequently ascribe the book *Laozi* to an author of the same name, but they provide neither credible details about his life nor any historical evidence that would have been sufficient proof of his existence.) Therefore, it was unknown what the *Laozi* had looked like before it went through the hands of Wang Bi. This situation changed when, in 1973, some quite spectacular archaeological discoveries were made in the southern Chinese province of Hunan. Close to a town called Mawangdui, several well-preserved tombs of local rulers from the time of the beginning of the Han Dynasty (206 BCE–220 CE) were found. Among the texts stored in the tombs were two early silk manuscripts of the *Laozi*, which have been dated around 200 BCE. Now, for the first time in many centuries, one can actually see a version of the *Laozi* that is nearly half a millennium older than the one edited by Wang Bi.

FIGURE 1
The Mawangdui Silk Manuscripts of the *Laozi*.

The Mawangdui silk manuscripts are, on the one hand, astonishingly similar to Wang Bi's edition: there are no essential discrepancies in content. Thus it is safe to say that Wang Bi's edition of the *Laozi* did indeed quite truly represent the text as it had existed more than 400 years before his lifetime. Nevertheless, there are, on the other hand, some remarkable differences between the early Han *Laozi* and the later version that has been known to us for so long. The Mawangdui silk manuscripts do not yet bear a title or an author's name, are not divided into eighty-one chapters—the text just "flows" from saying to saying with only traces of punctuation and division—and contain many words and characters (many with a mainly grammatical function) that were latter omitted. Moreover, the two sections of the *Dao-de-jing,* namely "Dao" (chapters 1–37 in the Wang Bi edition) and "De" (chapters 38–81 in the Wang Bi edition) appear in the reverse order.

While the reasons for the reversal of the two parts are unclear, it is highly probable that the text was later divided into *eighty-one* chapters because of the symbolical prestige attached to this number in ancient China: 81 is the power of the power of 3, and since 3 was a symbol of "simple" wholeness, 81 was perceived to symbolize a highly enriched and complex unity. Especially in later Han times, the *Laozi* was more and more held as a sort of "holy" revelation, and thus it made sense to have it assume a "geometrical" shape expressing its "wholeness." The shortening of the text can also be explained on the basis of its increasingly religious status: According to a widespread legend, Laozi's "original" version was comprised of 5000 characters. Since the earlier versions have a few hundred characters more, later editors obviously tried to "restore" its "authentic" shape.

Two decades after the Mawangdui discovery, new excavations aroused the interest of the scholars of Daoism: In 1993, near Guodian, a village in the province of Hubei, archeologists again found some manuscripts of the *Laozi* buried in an ancient aristocratic tomb. Several inscribed bamboo slips could be identified as early written records of sayings contained in the *Laozi.* Altogether, about two-fifths of what was to become the *Daodejing* were already present in these "bamboo fragments." The texts cannot as yet be dated as exactly as the Mawangdui manuscripts are, but experts agree that, at the latest, they stem back to the end of the fourth century BCE. Thus, the Guodian bamboo fragments are at least one century older than the Mawangdui *Laozi.*

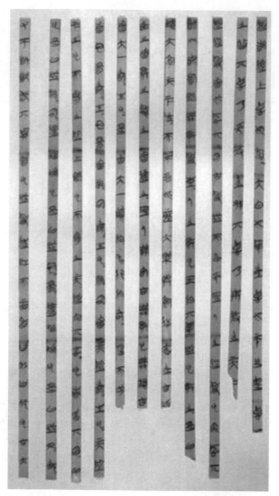

FIGURE 2
The Guodian Bamboo Manuscripts of the *Laozi*.

The manuscripts from Mawangdui and Guodian show that the
Laozi—or at least essential parts of it—already existed in the fourth
and third centuries BCE. No other widely known Daoist writing
can, without doubt, be traced back to such an early point in history. In this respect, one can indeed say that the history of Daoist
thought—as it is known today—begins with the *Laozi*.
Nevertheless, it is still not known exactly when and by whom the
text was "originally" written or composed.

The excavated manuscripts support the theory that the *Laozi* cannot be ascribed to a single, historically identifiable author, but that it is, instead, a collection of separate "philosophical" sayings that were transmitted orally before they were written down. This is strongly suggested by the distinctive style of the text. A great many of the sayings are rhymed, and the language is dense and highly "concentrated." Some of the sayings sound like an oracle, some of them like a riddle, and some seem to be ritual formulas. Obviously, the *Laozi* was meant to be learnt by heart, and it was spoken aloud and orally transmitted. It is likely that in the earliest years of its circulation, written copies of the text—like the manuscripts found in the tombs—were the exception rather than the rule. If one wanted to provide the dead with a version of the *Laozi*, it had to be in the form of a scripture—in life there was, however, no need for this.

If this theory about the origins of the *Laozi* is correct, the text is an anthology of wise sayings that were transmitted among the intellectual "elite" of ancient China, and it comprises materials from different sources and from different times. The earliest strata of the text may well be 2500 years old or more. The practice of putting artifacts and writings into the tombs of members of the aristocracy may have contributed to the increasing "literalization" of the *Laozi* and other "books." When writing became easier and more common (for instance, through the invention of paper during the Han dynasty), the present-day *Laozi* began to take shape. When this had happened, philosophers and literati like Wang Bi prepared their own editions of the text by adding commentaries and interpretations. At this point in history, the *Laozi* had ceased to be an orally transmitted collection of *sayings* and finally became a "classical scripture" known as the *Daode-jing*, which means: "The *Classical Scripture* (Chinese: *jing*) about Dao and De." Using a metaphor from the *Laozi*, one might say that over several centuries the *Laozi* had changed from "uncarved wood" into an elaborate wood carving. Thus, it is impossible to identify a single author who, at a specific point in history, composed the "authentic" *Daodejing*. It is rather a "collaborative" work that emerged within a philosophic tradition over a long period of time. There never was a person called Laozi who had "written" the text that was later given his name.

Although the excavated manuscripts strongly support the "orality" theory of the origins of the *Laozi* as a text, there are still attempts being made to identify a historical author. A main source for these attempts is the most important ancient Chinese work of history, the voluminous *The Grand Scribe's Records* (Chinese: *Shiji*) by Sima Qian (145–[86?] BCE), which contains a "biography" of Laozi.[2] This biography, like many others in the *Shiji*, mixes what appears to be historical information with obviously legendary and mythological materials. Among the relatively well-known legendary stories about Laozi recorded in this biography are reports about a meeting between him and Confucius (in which the latter asks the former for instruction), as well as the above-mentioned tale about the origin of the *Daodejing* "in 5000 characters." When the elderly Laozi decided to travel westwards (towards a presumed paradise located beyond the mountains), the frontier guard asked him not to leave the country without leaving behind his wisdom. Thus, the story goes, Laozi wrote the *Daodejing* in 5000 characters. Even though some Chinese researchers on Daoism still try to somehow connect this tale with history, it seems more likely that it is an etiological legend. When, in Sima Qian's times, writing had more and more replaced orality and the *Laozi* had been transformed into a scripture, there was now a need for finding an explanation of the origin of the *Laozi as a book*. Scriptures had become more prestigious than oral stories and sayings, and therefore, a prestigious text could no longer be without an original *writer*. By inventing an author and a legend of how the text was actually written, the *Laozi* was established both as a book and as an author.

While we are still in the dark about who had written—or rather, composed—the *Daodejing*, it is quite clear for whom—in the beginning—it was composed, namely for the political (and military) leaders of ancient China. (At the time of its "origins," China was factually divided into a multitude of "Warring States"—as this historical period is traditionally called.) The core topic of the *Daodejing* is the same as that of most other Chinese philosophical texts from this age: the order and rule of society. As a collection of sayings, the *Daodejing* offers advice to rulers for governing and ordering a state, such as in chapter 60: "Govern a big state like (you) fry a small fish!" (That is, without much ado.)

It is not easy to detect the political orientation of the *Daodejing* at first sight, because its language is not only formulaic and poetical, but also quite cryptic. However, a closer look often reveals that many statements that seem to be somewhat irritating at first are in fact rather straightforward strategic guidelines—just like the image of the rulers' "fish fry." Sometimes the *Daodejing* literally addresses the "ruler," but more often it speaks to the "sage" (Chinese: *sheng ren*). But in ancient China the "sage" was, ideally, supposed to be the ruler, so that in fact these two designations do not essentially differ. When the *Daodejing* speaks about the sage, it means (or at least it meant at the time when it was composed) the *sage ruler*.

That the Daodejing was addressed to rulers can be inferred not only from its content (and from the fact that it was put into the tombs of aristocrats), but also from some of its stylistic features. When the word "I" appears in the text, this "I" is not the "ego" of an individual author or of a certain wise man or woman, but rather the "I" of the envisioned reader, or rather listener. It is the "I" of the prospective ruler who studies the teaching of the *Daodejing*. This "I" functions similar to the "I" as it was used some time ago, for instance, in "educational" materials for children where one could find sentences like: "I brush my teeth at least twice a day." It is an "I" that asks the reader or listener to identify him/herself with, and not the "I" of the speaker or of the author. A poetically impressive chapter of the *Daodejing* that uses the "I" in such a way is chapter 20. This chapter contrasts the ruler and the ruled, and it says: "The ordinary people are shining / I alone seem to be hidden." It is suggested here that the reader/listener identifies him/herself with the "I" in the text and will follow a Daoist guideline for good government: The ideal ruler will hardly "come to the fore." Since he or she acts "without acting" he or she is hardly perceived. As opposed to the ruled, the good ruler is practically invisible.

The *Daodejing* was, historically speaking, at first a thoroughly political work. The oldest known commentary to some of its chapters is incorporated in an ancient Chinese "classic" of "political theory" called the *Hanfeizi* (which is named after its prominent Legalist author).[3] Daoist thought first developed and became influential within the context of political thought. The political dimension of early Daoist thought manifested itself in the so-called philosophy of "Huang-Lao-Daoism," which was an important political teaching in the second century BCE (see pages 12–14 below).

In accordance with the political dimension of early Daoism, the notions of "Dao" and "De" can be understood in a political sense. The Dao as a "Way" (which is the literal translation of the Chinese term *dao*)—or more specifically, as the best way of "proceeding" or of "going on"—was in early Daoism more often than not the "Way of Government" (See part II, 1 below for details). One who understands the *Dao* of government, and who knows how to order society in the most effective "Way," will be able to bring about the unfolding of a great social *efficacy* or "power"—which is how one can translate *De*, the second word in the title of the *Dao-De-Jing*. *De* is the power or efficacy that a perfectly ordered or governed (social) "process" (i.e., a "Way" or *Dao*) displays. This is the reason the book of *Laozi* was called the *Daodejing*: "The Classical Scripture of the Way and Its Efficacy."

The *Zhuangzi*

Daoist philosophy was by no means restricted to teaching the art of government. Even though the *Daodejing* was initially meant to be a sort of guidebook for prospective rulers, it was nevertheless cryptic enough to provoke interpretations that far exceeded the realm of the political. The vision of a perfectly ordered society that this work presented was from the beginning intrinsically connected with a vision of a perfectly ordered world, with a perfect order of "heaven, earth, and man." While in the *Daodejing* the order of society is a starting point for many philosophical considerations, this did not exclude wider horizons. In a certain sense, Daoist philosophy can be understood, in analogy to ancient Greek "metaphysics," as a kind of "meta-politics." Whereas some ancient Greek philosophers tried to understand and describe those dimensions that go "beyond" (*meta-*) the "merely" physical, some ancient Daoists went beyond a focus on political order and tried to widen the scope of their reflections to include some broader or more "fundamental" issues.

While a general "meta-political" philosophical reflection on issues such as life and death is latently present in the *Daodejing*, it is much more obvious and explicit in the second core text of ancient Daoism: the *Zhuangzi*. The *Zhuangzi* is most likely not as old as the *Daodejing*—or at least not as old as many of the materials contained in the latter, such as those found in Guodian. Thus the *Zhuangzi* can be understood as a further development of Daoist philosophy. In the *Zhuangzi* the political aspects of Daoist philosophy are not only thrust into the background, but oftentimes ridiculed and satirized. The Daoism of the *Zhuangzi* is no longer about politics, it is rather about how to live—and how to die.

Despite its philosophical importance, the *Zhuangzi* is—especially in the West—somewhat less recognized and well-known than the *Daodejing*. This might in part be due to the immense difficulties it poses to any translation (even into modern Chinese). Unlike the *Daodejing*, the *Zhuangzi* does not consist of an array of loosely related concise sayings, but is instead a complex mixture of poetic allegories, of rhymed verse, of short treatises and sometimes lengthy dialogues on philosophical issues, and of anecdotes about often legendary or even fairy-tale-like "creatures"—to mention only some of the literary features found in it. And unlike the *Daodejing*, which is quite short, the *Zhuangzi* is a rather voluminous book. It stands out as a very special piece of literature in its times and culture—many of its poetic devices, such as speaking animals, and, most importantly, its extensive use of puns and irony distinguish it strongly in style from most other writings of ancient China.

The unique writing style of the *Zhuangzi* is paralleled by a likewise unique "style of thinking." Whereas some other ancient Chinese "meta-political" texts, such as the *Daodejing* (or even more, the *Yijing*, the "Book of Changes"), tend to evoke an aura of mysticism by a terse and nebulous way of expression, the *Zhuangzi* presents its readers with many straightforward stories and reflections. However, allegories that at first appear to be simple may well turn out to be multilayered images of a tricky philosophical train of thought; tales that start off rather uncomplicated may end with an astonishing twist, and seemingly unproblematic contemplations may soon leave one startled and perplexed. The philosophical meaning is not dissolved in a diffuse "depth"— instead the unpretentious but profound language shakes the foundations of common sense and challenges the reader's reasoning.

Like the *Daodejing*, the *Zhuangzi* was not written by a single author at a specific time. The various theories about the origin of the text agree that its present-day version is a compendium of different textual segments that stem from different sources. The oldest layer of the text might indeed go back to a philosopher named Zhuang Zhou, that is, the Zhuangzi, or "Master Zhuang," after whom the book was named. Zhuang Zhou is supposed to have lived from 369 BCE to 286 BCE, and could have been the author of the first seven of the text's thirty-three chapters altogether. Even in ancient China it is clear that these first seven chapters were perceived to represent the core of the work since they were traditionally grouped together as the "inner chapters." The seven "inner chapters" are followed by the fifteen "outer chapters" and by the eleven "mixed chapters."

Sinologists generally believe that some portions of the "outer" and "mixed" chapters were composed by immediate followers or later students of Zhuang Zhou. In addition, materials from other Daoist schools of thought seem to have been integrated into the work. These other schools include the Daoist "primitivists," who relied upon some passages from the *Daodejing* to advocate a very simple and ascetic lifestyle; the "syncretists," who combined a variety of Daoist and non-Daoist ideas; and the school of the legendary Daoist "maverick" Yang Zhu, who is said to have lived in the fifth century BCE and was primarily concerned with the intactness of his body.

Textual predecessors of the present-day *Zhuangzi* most likely existed as early as the second century BCE. The above mentioned historical *Grand Scribe's Records* not only mention Laozi, but also contain information about Zhuang Zhou. It states that he followed in the philosophical footsteps of Laozi and authored a couple of writings.[4] About two centuries later, an imperial book catalogue (which is preserved in the *History of the Han Dynasty* or *Hanshu*, a historical compendium of the first century CE) lists a work entitled the *Zhuangzi* that consisted of fifty-two chapters. These two sources show that a book named or ascribed to Zhuangzi existed in the Han Dynasty. However, none of these texts have been transmitted as such and—unlike the case of the *Daodejing*—no excavations have brought any early manuscripts to light.

The version of the *Zhuangzi* that we have today, and to which Western translations refer, is a rather idiosyncratic edition of the text by the philosopher Guo Xiang (d. 312 CE). Guo Xiang (probably continuing the work of others before him) newly collated and commented on the work. He revised the division of the text by shortening it to thirty-three chapters (instead of the fifty-two the

Han catalogue recorded), and his edition of the text—even though
other commentaries and editions have continually appeared—
remains the standard version of the *Zhuangzi*. In the course of his
revision, Guo Xiang obviously rearranged, altered, and even
deleted many passages. He might also have added some material.
Most importantly, he inserted his own extensive philosophical
commentaries into the text (which was common practice in ancient
China; the commentary continuously interrupts the text and frequently exceeds the commented passages in length). Guo Xiang
blended his interpretation into the *Zhuangzi* and thus shaped it
into a more or less coherent unit. He molded text and commentary together, and what emerged is an incessant and often insepa-
rable (though always fascinating) dialogue between text and
commentary.

The book of *Zhuangzi* as it exists today is therefore a creation
of the fourth-century philosopher Guo Xiang based on the materials of its Han Dynasty (or even older) versions. Guo Xiang's commentary is by no means a mere explanation of the older "original"
text. The older materials were employed as a kind of framework
used by Guo to introduce his own philosophical reflections.
Therefore the Chan Buddhist (or in Japanese: the Zen Buddhist)
Zonggao (1089–1163 CE) remarked correctly: "It is always presumed that Guo Xiang commented on Zhuangzi, but one who
understands will say that it is Zhuangzi who comments on Guo
Xiang."[5]

Unfortunately, only a minor part of Guo Xiang's commentary
on the *Zhuangzi* is available in English translation—and the little
that is, is not easily accessible. Many English translations of the
Zhuangzi tend to ignore Guo Xiang's editorial input and philosophical commentary and therefore present the Western reader
with a somewhat limited view of the philosophical and poetical
richness of the text. This is especially the case with some early
translations that became quite influential among Western intellectuals of the twentieth century. The translation by H. A. Giles (first
published in 1889) proved to be especially effective in imprinting
a relatively distorted image of the *Zhuangzi* in the mind of its
modern readership. Even though this rendering was certainly a
major Sinological effort at its time, it is not very faithful to the
original and often suffers from a "Westernization" of its concepts.
Because of its elaborate and very readable style, it made its way not

only into the bookshelves of important English language authors, such as Oscar Wilde and Henry Miller, but through the mediation of its famous and not so famous readership, some of its allegories and tales (like the "Dream of the Butterfly") became rather well known in the West—even though not everyone who heard these stories knew where they actually came from.

In the philosophical world, H.A. Giles's translation was even more "successful." The renowned Jewish philosopher and theologian Martin Buber (1878–1965) published a widely read selection of "the allegories and parables of Zhuangzi" by translating passages from Giles's translation into German. This—again very elegantly written, but even more "Westernized" or rather "Juadaeo-Christianized" version—was for many decades a main source for knowledge about the *Zhuangzi* and Daoism in the West and it notably influenced, for instance, the eminent philosopher Martin Heidegger (1899–1976) and the likewise eminent writer Hermann Hesse. On the one hand, translations like those by Giles and Buber made the *Zhuangzi* palatable to Western readers and contributed considerably to making Daoism known as a "serious" world philosophy. On the other hand, however, such translations have established some rather uniform and often misleading perceptions of the text and philosophy of the *Zhuangzi*. In part I of this book I will attempt to present some readings and translations of allegories from the *Zhuangzi* in the light of a more "original" context—namely, in the light of Guo Xiang's commentary—in the hope of expressing a more truly Daoist explanation of the philosophy of the *Zhuangzi*.

Huang-Lao-Daoism

"Huang-Lao-Daoism" is a very old designation that only recently gained a new recognition among scholars of Chinese philosophy. Quite contrary to the *Zhuangzi*, which ventures far beyond the *Daodejing*'s concern for political issues, Huang-Lao-Daoism represents an effort to focus more specifically on a Daoist theory of political action (or rather political action through "nonaction"). Around 200 BCE, when the Han Dynasty succeeded the short-lived Empire of the Qin, Huang-Lao-Daoism became influential at the imperial court, and many of the early Han rulers seem to have been followers of this teaching.

The expression Huang-Lao-Daoism refers on the one hand to *Huang*-di (literally, the "Yellow Emperor"), a legendary ancient ruler who was revered as an ideal monarch and a founding father of Chinese civilization. On the other hand, it refers to *Lao*-zi, the legendary author of the *Daodejing*. The fact that the term Huang-Lao-Daoism relates a legendary political figure to a legendary philosopher clearly demonstrates the strong political inclination of this school of thought.

Notwithstanding its considerable importance at the early stages of the Chinese imperial period, Huang-Lao-Daoism was soon philosophically marginalized and was more and more neglected. Its decline was manifested by the loss of many of its core texts. Only in recent years has Sinological research rediscovered this type of Daoism, and a major reason for this resurgence were the excavations of Mawangdui. Next to the aforementioned versions of the *Daodejing*, the silk manuscripts of Mawangdui contained one of the central writings of Huang-Lao-Daoism that had been lost for many centuries. This text had been directly attached to one of the versions of the *Daodejing*, and most Sinological researchers agree that it is to be identified as the *Four Classics of the Yellow Emperor* or *Huangdi sijing*, which is referred to in several Han Dynasty writings.[6]

Huang-Lao-Daoism translates the teachings of the *Daodejing* into a forthright method of how to become or be a sovereign. (Because of this political orientation some Sinologists in fact suggest we understand the Huang-Lao school not as branch of Daoism, but rather as a variation of Confucianism.) Like Hanfeizi in his Legalist treatise, Huang-Lao-Daoism introduces many Daoist precepts as aspects of a technique for government. A single ruler is supposed to exercise the power of the Dao. He is supposed to refrain from action and thus gives way to the natural unfolding of the rule of the Dao. Instead of actively interfering in matters of government, he has only to supervise the harmony of "forms and names": The "names" are the designations of offices, professions, and social roles, and it is believed that these provide for a kind of natural order of society. If people will only per*form* or act according with these *names*, then "forms and names" are in correspondence. The ruler's duty is to make everybody else embody his or her "name." If everybody acts in accordance with his or her "natural" designation, the Dao will prevail and the state will flourish.

It is not only the central role of "nonaction" (*wu wei*) that shows the Daoist origins of the Huang-Lao teaching. Many other expressions can be traced back to the *Daodejing* and its metaphorics. The "Four Classics of the Yellow Emperor," for instance, admonish the ruler to hold on to a "female" (*ci jie*) or a "soft" (*ruo jie*) practice of retreating and restraining himself. Images like these prove the close relation between the Huang-Lao scriptures and major Daoist "classics."

The recovery of the *Four Classics of the Yellow Emperor* allows for the identification of elements of the Huang-Lao doctrine in several other texts from ancient China. Works like the *Guanzi*[7] and the *Huainanzi*[8] are compilations that stem back to a variety of different sources and have a long and complex history of transmission. These texts have always been recognized as containing a wide range of Daoist teachings; they are, however, even more heterogeneous in content and style than the *Daodejing*, the *Zhuangzi*, and the *Four Classics of the Yellow Emperor*. Now it is possible to discern obvious traces of the political philosophy of Huang-Lao-Daoism within these textual collections.

Daoist Mysticism

Historically speaking, the school of "Daoist Mysticism" represents the final blossoming of Daoist philosophy in the time before Buddhism penetrated and transformed Chinese culture and thought. The Chinese term for this leading philosophical trend in the third and fourth century CE is *xuan xue*, which literally means something like "the teaching of the dark" or the "school of the hidden." (The same expression was later used to translate the Western term "metaphysics.") This designation was derived from a verse in the first chapter of the *Daodejing* which "mystically" describes the Dao as "darker than dark" or "more hidden than hidden" (*xuan zhi you xuan*).

Contrary to the "classical" Daoism of the *Laozi*, and the *Zhuangzi*, and also to Huang-Lao-Daoism, the most important extant sources of the Neo-Daoists are not individual writings or books. Instead, we know about them and their thought primarily through the commentaries they wrote on earlier philosophical masterpieces, through some stories about them that can be found in the literature of their era, and through a few short treatises on philosophical issues that were recorded in later compilations. The two most prominent Neo-Daoists have already been mentioned above: Wang Bi (226–249 CE) and Guo Xiang (d. 312 CE). Wang Bi's commentary on the *Daodejing* and Guo Xiang's commentary on the *Zhuangzi* lead to a new philosophical understanding of these two most important Daoist classics. Wang's and Guo's commentaries and editions have so much influenced the interpretations of the earlier scriptures that it has subsequently become extremely difficult—particularly in the case of Guo Xiang and the *Zhuangzi*—to reconstruct the meaning, and even the text itself, as it was before their treatment of it.

Wang Bi was renowned not only for his knowledge of Daoist philosophy, but also for his studies of the *Analects* of Confucius and the *Book of Changes* (*Yijing*). However, it is certain that, historically, his most influential achievement was his edition of the *Daodejing*. In his commentary on the text he developed a nearly "metaphysical" concept of the core Daoist notion of "emptiness" or "nothingness" (Chinese: *wu*). Wang Bi understood this notion, which is intrinsically connected with the notion of the Dao, in the sense of an ultimate origin of all beings and things. Commenting on the first chapter of the *Daodejing*, Wang Bi writes: "Everything which is there begins from nothingness [*wu*]. Therefore, the time when there were yet no shapes and no names was the beginning of the ten thousand things."[9] This time, or this "nothingness" or "emptiness," can be identified with the Dao, as Wang Bi states in his commentary on the fifty-first chapter: "The Dao—this is where things come from." And in regard to the twenty-fifth chapter, he says: "It is spoken of as 'Dao' [i.e.: as 'Way'] insofar as there is thus something [for things] to come from." This interpretation of the Dao as both "nothingness" and a kind of "origin for all things" has paved the way for later "metaphysical" interpretations of Daoism as a teaching about a specific force of "creation." I personally believe that such a "metaphysical" perception of the Dao—which might indeed have been on Wang Bi's mind—does not lead one very far in understanding the philosophical "essence" of the *Daodejing*, and may even obstruct an insight into the exciting "nonmetaphysical" aspects of Daoist thought.[10]

Guo Xiang's edition of *Zhuangzi* is, as I see it, a much more original contribution to Daoist philosophy—"original" both in the sense of being in line with the "origins" of Daoist philosophy and of being a unique and inventive transformation of those origins. In contrast to Wang Bi's somewhat pompous and static reification of the Dao and its nothingness as the founding stone of the creation of things, Guo Xiang brings to light the more subtle and dynamic elements of Daoist thinking. The latter opposes an interpretation of both the Dao and the teaching of the *Zhuangzi* as an account of cosmological creation or as a solution to a metaphysical question. He rather develops a complex philosophy of "in-difference" and "equal validity" (for instance of cause and effect, and of origin and result). For Guo Xiang, the Daoist philosophical quest is surely not one for an ultimate "origin." He writes: "If one traces [things] back to what they depend on and searches for where they come from, then tracing and searching will have no end until one reaches the non-dependent and the pattern of change-alone becomes clear."[11]

A main source for stories about the protagonists of the "Mystical Teaching" of Neo-Daoism is a collection of quaint anecdotes and pointed debates which was compiled in the fifth century CE under the title *A New Account of Tales of the World* (*Shishuo xinyu*).[12] Unfortunately, the philosophical materials contained in this book are so terse and dispersed that it is difficult to fit them together into a coherent philosophical picture.

One of the most important Neo-Daoist treatises on philosophical issues is a brief essay by the philosopher He Yan (d. 249 CE), which is entitled "On the Nameless" (*Wuming lun*).[13] Similar to Wang Bi, He Yan did not only study and contribute to Daoist philosophy, but also worked on Confucian texts. He wrote a commentary to the *Analects*, and it is specifically this commentary that secured him a place in the history of Chinese thought.

Daoist Practice

Historical sources indicate that an institutionalized Daoist practice—or, as it is sometimes called, "Daoist religion"[14]— begins later than Daoist philosophy, namely not earlier than the second century CE. Still, many important elements of Daoist practice have a much longer history. A core concern of (early) Daoist practice was the search for immortality and longevity. This very aim was, most notably, already pursued in vain by the notorious "First Emperor of Qin" (*Qin Shi Huangdi*—the emperor whose tomb, near the present-day city of Xian, is protected by the world-famous terra cotta army) in the third century BCE. Within a Daoist context, the quest for immortality is directly related to an ideal that figures very prominently: the ideal of a permanent and unimpeded functioning or order of things that acts in perfect harmony with the Dao. Many Daoists believed that if one was only able to organize one's physical body in accordance with the Dao, then it could be as everlasting and imperishable as the ideal state envisioned in the *Daodejing*.

Other characteristic features of Daoist practice have early predecessors as well: breathing techniques and practices of meditation are alluded to in the *Zhuangzi*; early Chinese folk religion had elaborate ideas about the functioning of the cosmos and its powers and spirits; and there existed astonishingly bureaucratic conceptions of an underworld. Daoism combined and unified such practices and beliefs,[15] and it turned the legendary Laozi into a god. An interesting scripture in this regard is a treatise called the *Classic of the Transformations of Laozi* (*Laozi bianhua jing*). This text, which seems to have been written in the second century CE, portrays Laozi as a kind of a creator-god. However, in typical Daoist fashion, this creator-god by no means transcends the world by dwelling in a realm far beyond it; rather, he continuously stays within it. He takes part in many earthly activities by adopting a multitude of physical shapes. Sometimes he appears as a wise consultant of a ruler, and sometimes as a practitioner absorbed in Daoist meditation. In this way, even the historical Buddha has at times been seen as one of the transformations of the godly Laozi after he had left China and went West.

The deification of Laozi was certainly an important step towards the establishment of an institutionalized Daoist practice, but the formation of a Daoist movement with a specific organization was equally significant. While a deified Laozi could serve as a unifying image for the integration of various elements of folk religion with different philosophical and political teachings, there was still the need for a social association in order to actually bind people together as a community. Only in this way could a religion in the strict sense of the term really "take off": A more or less coherent amalgamation of beliefs and practices had to go along with the creation of a group of people who identified themselves as a common body of followers.

Religious groups need not only gods or objects to worship, but also leaders to socially connect the believers. In this way, Daoist practice began in the second century CE as a popular movement guided by people who were inspired by Daoist ideas. The history of an institutionalized Daoist practice begins, so to speak, with its first preacher. As far as the sources can tell us, this was a man named Zhang Daoling who had seen Laozi in a divine vision during the year 142 CE. Zhang Daoling was to become the founding father of the first Daoist "church," the group of the so-called Celestial Masters (*tianshi*).[16] Even today there are Daoists who hold that they are descendants of this group. Under the leadership of Zhang Daoling's grandson Zhang Lu (approx. 190–220), the early Daoist church of the Celestial Masters developed into a kind of semiautonomous political entity in a relatively remote area of China located in the present-day province of Sichuan. The early Celestial Masters were also known as the "Five Pecks of Rice Sect" (*Wudou mi dao*) because the members of the community had to pay this amount of rice as a tax. This nickname well illustrates that by this time at the latest, Daoism was no longer a mere philosophical "theory," but had developed into social organizations with an economic and political structure.

From this time on, Daoism brought forth a vast multitude of communities and along with those a vast multitude of texts and practices. The introduction of Buddhism into China had an especially strong influence on the further development of Daoist practice. Buddhism had brought with it certain institutional structures that had been unknown or uncommon in China. In many ways the history of Daoist practice runs parallel to the history of Buddhism in China. Following Buddhist models, Daoists established a canon of scriptures, founded monasteries based on master-disciple relations, and created a specific pantheon. Since the second century CE Daoist practice has always been a major element within Chinese society and culture, and in some periods—for instance during the Tang Dynasty (618–907 CE)—even a dominating factor.

Daoism Today

Daoism continues to live on in different but overlapping forms: as a practice, as a philosophy, and as an object of cultural preservation and academic research.

Daoism is practiced in monasteries and/or communities in the People's Republic of China, in Hong Kong (which is politically part of the People's Republic again), in Taiwan, and among the Chinese population of Southeast Asia and elsewhere. Although Daoism was repressed on the mainland—specifically during the communist "Cultural Revolution" in the 1960s and '70s—there is a certain revival taking place. The present Chinese government has recognized the role of "traditional" Chinese religions for the (re-)shaping of a national "identity" and now looks much more sympathetically at Daoism (and, more particularly, at Confucianism). These traditions are more and more accepted by the government as integral parts of the cultural heritage of China, while foreign religions (such as Christianity), and new practices (such as Falungong), are still not welcomed by the Communist rulers. Daoist sites on the mainland are becoming increasingly popular, not only as tourism spots, but also as places of worship. In Hong Kong and Taiwan, Daoism had never ceased to be an important element of society and is still very much alive as a religion today—as mentioned above, Taiwan is still home to the Celestial Masters.[17]

Like Buddhism, Daoism has become ever more fashionable in the "West," particularly in North America and Western Europe, but also to a certain degree in South America and Eastern Europe. Here, it is often the case that Daoist beliefs or practices are mixed with other Eastern and Western ideas or techniques so that new and peculiar usages of the "Dao" have become rather widespread—as is manifested in numerous book or film titles beginning with the "The Dao of. . . ." Generally speaking, traditional Chinese exercises such as *Qigong*, *Taiji quan*, and *Wushu* (martial arts) have now firmly established themselves within the multicultural pattern of Western society and culture. These bodily and spiritual practices tend to incorporate Daoist ingredients in various quantities.

Daoist philosophy was somewhat marginalized in China after the heyday of Neo-Daoism in the third and fourth century CE. To be sure, throughout Chinese history the Daoist philosophical "classics" such as the *Daodejing* and the *Zhuangzi* were continuously studied and exerted an immense influence on Chinese intellectuals and thus also on the development of both Confucian and Buddhist philosophy, but, unlike these philosophies, no new great masters emerged. In other words: Daoist philosophy did not pro-

duce a Zhu Xi (1130–1200 CE) or a Dogen (1200–1253 CE)—
to name two people who greatly contributed to philosophical
developments in Confucianism and Buddhism and whose writings
(such as Zhu Xi's edition of the "Four Books" of Confucianism
and Dogen's *Shobogenzo*) gained the status of new "classics" within
their respective traditions.

In the twentieth century a new interest in Daoist *philosophy*
began to develop. This was first of all an effect of the attempt of
"Westernized" Chinese intellectuals to understand their own past
in terms of the Western notion of "philosophy." Once Western
science and thought—in the wake of the imperialism of the nine-
teenth century—inevitably confronted Chinese society, China
had to "compete." One way of competing was to (re-)interpret
the Chinese cultural heritage with Western means. Thus, Chinese
thinkers began to discover Chinese "natural science," Chinese
"political theory," and even some kind of Chinese Christianity—
all these categories which had never existed in traditional China.
When the Chinese took up the work of reconstructing a history
of philosophy, Daoism was recognized as one of the central con-
tributions of Chinese thought. However, Buddhism and especially Confucianism were taken up as the main pillars for building
a modernized Chinese philosophy. The most successful attempt
to rejuvenate traditional Chinese thought was—and still is—the
school of New Confucianism (*Xin rujia*). This school (which is
in many ways comparable to the Japanese "New Buddhist"
Kyoto School) tried to transform Confucianism into a modern
philosophy by systematizing it in a Western way and by expressing it in terms of a new "Westernized" language and in comparison with Western philosophers. The New Confucianists hoped
to preserve the "essence" of Chinese philosophy and culture, but
tried to mold it into a new form that would enable it to enter
twentieth-century global philosophical discourse—and hopefully
play a major role not only in future Chinese but in world society.
Whereas some New Confucianists such as Xiong Shili
(1883–1968) and Mou Zongsan (1909–1995) borrowed exten-
sively from Buddhist philosophy, others like Feng Youlan
(1895–1990) were interested in Daoism. Thus some New
Confucianists were also "New Buddhists," while Feng Youlan
may fairly—at least to a certain degree—be called the first modern New Daoist.

Feng Youlan (who was a student of John Dewey and received his doctoral degree in philosophy from Columbia University, New York, in 1924) is perhaps best known in the West for his monumental two-volume *History of Chinese Philosophy*, which has been translated into English. He also published a partial English translation of the *Zhuangzi* that includes some of the commentaries by Guo Xiang. Still largely untranslated are his own philosophical works, most importantly his six-book series on his "New Metaphysics" first published in the late 1930s and early 1940s.[18] Feng was especially interested in the "mystical" dimension of Daoist philosophy. His own system of thought consists of two parts or "methods"—a first and preliminary "positive" method of thinking that eventually has to be overcome by a "negative" one. Feng's positive method is rooted in the Confucian (and Western Platonic) tradition, while his negative method is basically a new version of Chan-Buddhist and particularly Daoist philosophy. He calls Chan-Buddhism and Daoism "philosophies of silence" that replace the Confucian discourse once it reaches the point where its "rationalism" becomes self-contradictory.

In Feng's view, the "rationalisms" of both Western and Eastern philosophy—represented by Platonism and Confucianism, respectively—end in a paradox: "each of these approaches arrives in its own way at a 'something' which logically is not the object of reason and therefore refuses to be analyzed by it. This is not because reason is weak, but because the 'something' is such that a rational analysis of it involves a logical contradiction."[19] Feng observed that "rational" attempts at constructing a complete or definite ontology or metaphysics typically arrived at some final "somethings" or Archemedian concepts that are in themselves no longer rationally analyzable. (Concepts like, for instance, "matter" or "God.") The Eastern and Western philosophical analyses of the realm of the knowable, according to Feng, lead inevitably to indications of a second realm of the unknowable. This calamity of rationalist metaphysics therefore, again according to Feng, lead to similar epistemological consequences both in the West and in the East, namely to a philosophical turn towards dealing with the issue of a "something" that in principle and by definition cannot be known. Feng says that Kantianism in the West and Daoism in the East represent this "negative" epistemological answer to the crisis of positive metaphysics. But, he also believes that Daoist philosophy—the philosophy of silence and of nothingness—supercedes

the Kantian effort. While Kantianism, when it reaches the boundaries of pure reason, stops short of crossing the line separating
knowledge from the "thing-in-itself," the Daoists managed,
according to Feng, to "cross the boundary with pure reason and
went to the other side, as it were." Using an intriguing metaphor,
Feng characterizes the Daoist "super-rationality" as follows: "the
negation of reason is itself an act of reason, just as a man committing suicide kills himself by his own acts."[20]

Feng Youlan insists that Daoism and his own "New Daoist"
philosophy are neither "irrational" or "a-rational," but rather
"trans-rational." In his view, Daoist mysticism is the "suicide" *of
rationality*, that is, the necessary final rational step of rationality
itself. It is the self-overcoming of rationalism.[21] With this self-overcoming, according to Feng, "there is no longer a boundary to
cross" and "nothing to distinguish."[22] Thus he comes to the
rational *and* mystical realization that "one cannot say what it is,
but only what it is not" and that "there is nothing to say and that
what one has to do is to be silent."[23] This is to him the essence of
Daoist mysticism and of his own "negative method" of philosophy.

For Feng, Daoism provided the answer not only to the paradoxes of Confucian philosophy, but also to those of Western
rationality. Feng strongly affirmed both Confucianism and
Western rational thinking, but he believed that these modes of
thought were in need of completion by Daoist philosophy. This is
what he meant when he wrote: "It seems to me that the future
world philosophy must be more rationalistic than the traditional
Chinese philosophy, and more mystical than the traditional
Western philosophy. Only a union of rationalism and mysticism
will make a philosophy worthy of the one world of the future."[24]

Readers familiar with Western philosophy may have already
wondered about the strange affinities between Feng Youlan's synthesis of rationalism and mysticism which leads to a philosophy of
silence and the young Ludwig Wittgenstein's *Tractatus logico-
philosophicus*. Feng was indeed well acquainted with Wittgenstein's
Tractatus, and he quotes the last paragraphs of this book, which
end with the famous statement "What we cannot speak about we
must pass over in silence," in his own seminal work *Xin Zhiyan* (*A
New Treatise on the Methodology of Metaphysics* or simply *New
Methodology*).[25] The *Tractatus* had been translated into Chinese as
early as 1927,[26] and Wittgenstein's philosophy, along with the

thought of the related Vienna Circle, was widely discussed among Chinese intellectuals in the 1930s. In fact, Feng Youlan met Wittgenstein in 1933 at Oxford where they shared a cup of tea and an afternoon conversation.[27] As is obvious from Feng's *New Methodology*, he believed that he (in China) and Wittgenstein (in the West) were part of a new development in "world philosophy" which was contributing to a resolution of the crisis of metaphysics by constructing different versions of a New Daoist philosophy of silence.[28]

At the time when the eminent Chinese philosopher Feng Youlan tried to revive Daoist "mysticism" in order to construct a new world philosophy, similar attempts were made by a foremost Western philosopher, albeit in a more secretive manner. Recent scholarship has proven and documented in detail how and where Martin Heidegger, one of the most influential thinkers of the twentieth century, heavily drew on Daoist sources.[29] Heidegger's interest in Asian thought, particularly in Zen Buddhism and Daoism, goes back to the early stages of his career, but it seems to have been an even more important contributing factor to his so-called "turn" or *Kehre*. Heidegger's later conceptions of Nothingness and his means of expressing these conceptions, particularly his use of the image of the jug[30] (illustrating the centrality of nothingness or emptiness), seem to be derived directly from the *Daodejing*. Indeed, in 1946 Heidegger had himself attempted to translate this work into German with the help of a Chinese colleague.[31] Heidegger rarely publicly acknowledged his intensive study of Asian, and particularly Daoist, thought and seldom openly referred to them in his written works.[32] Therefore it is difficult to assess exactly how much of a Daoist Heidegger believed himself to be. Nevertheless it is clear that he took Daoist philosophy seriously, that he not only knew but also deeply reflected on the *Daodejing* and the *Zhuangzi*,[33] and that his thought integrated core elements of their philosophy.

The examples of Feng Youlan and Martin Heidegger, key intellectual figures of the twentieth century in China and the West, show that Daoist philosophy is very much alive in our time. This fact is also reflected by the large number of translations, especially of the *Daodejing*, into Western languages and by its inclusion in elementary philosophy textbooks. Today, Daoism is, culturally speaking, a "global player"; it influences the art and architecture, the poetry and music, the religious practice and the intellectual life of the whole world. However, what Daoist philosophy actually and concretely means is often still only vaguely understood. This present book is an attempt to clarify the meaning of Daoist philosophy, that is, both its sense and its significance.

The Dao

This glance at the history of Daoism, and particularly of Daoist philosophy, shall be concluded with a brief look at the core notion of Daoism—the "Dao." It is intended to provide the reader with a first impression of what the rest of the book is about.

The notion of the Dao is less a descriptive one than a prescriptive one, less explanatory than advisory. Ancient Chinese philosophy in general, and Daoism in particular, tends to be somewhat focused on results or success; it tends to be more, so to speak, "effect-centered" than "truth-centered." A main concern was to develop efficient strategies and behavioral patterns. Therefore, more attention was directed towards questions of how certain goals could be achieved than towards questions about the "true essence" of things.

The *Daodejing* shows that at least in the early stages of Daoism issues such as the order and effective organization both of one's own body and of the social community were of central importance. These issues were directly related to political matters such as diplomacy or warfare. Order and organization in the political realm were also believed to be in direct correspondence to order and organization in nature and in the cosmos. The world of culture or of civilization was an intimate part of the natural world, or rather, there was no border drawn between nature and culture. Instead of such a distinction, one common order was believed to unite social and celestial space. Social ceremonies, the organization of the state, and the rules of the mainly agrarian economy sought to be in correspondence with astronomical and astrological patterns and in harmony with the religious prescriptions of ancestor worship. The vision of order was projected from a macrocosmic dimension to a microcosmic one. Just as social order was conceived to be analogous to and in concordance with cosmic order, the cultivation of the individual body resulting in health, and particularly in longevity, was believed to be an effect or an expression of the same order.

In the context of a philosophy focusing on order and efficacy, the Dao or the "Way" was an expression of a scenario for ultimate order and ideal effects. Accordingly, there was a multitude of Daos in ancient Chinese philosophy: the Dao of heaven, of earth, of man, but also of government or of warfare. Next to all these specific conceptions of perfect ways, there was also the Dao or the Way as such, the idea of a perfect order for all proceedings, a sort of way of all ways, a method of all methods, a pattern of all patterns.

As opposed to some popular treatments today, such as in books describing the Dao of this or that, dealing with one or the general Dao in ancient China was the privilege of a cultural and political elite. The "dispute of the Dao" provided the vocabulary in which the educated and the powerful argued about how to act and the language in which they explained society and the world to themselves. In ancient China, the Dao was by no means the exclusive term of the Daoists. It was a guiding concept for all philosophical schools, and everyone who intended to take part in intellectual debates had to be able to discuss it.

The Dao or the Way shows how something goes well. The Dao of Daoist philosophy—as I am hoping to be able to show in this book—shows the same, but on the basis of a specific, continuously varied structure. The structure of the Daoist Way is built upon only two elements: "Being" and "Nothingness," or, more concretely, Emptiness and Fullness, or, more technically, Presence and Nonpresence. Before I begin unearthing this structure in a number of Daoist images, allegories, and philosophical conceptions, I will try to explain it with an example that has not much to do with ancient China, but concerns current Western culture. The psychologist Mihaly Csikszentmihaly has coined the term "flow experience."[34] While doing certain activities, people stop consciously realizing that they are actually performing them. The activity seems to go on just by itself and the actor experiences some kind of a "lightness of being." This can happen, for instance, while jogging. One runs and runs, and at a certain point one ceases to feel any effort; the body seems to be running smoothly and easily by itself. In such a case something occurs that bears a resemblance to what the Daoists believed to be happening when a scenario of the Dao is established: While on the one hand the "ego" of the runner disappears and is, so to speak, emptied, the running itself, on the other hand, becomes an effortless, continuous, and perfectly functioning going-on. This is the combination of emptiness and fullness or of nonpresence and presence that is at the core of the Daoist way. Once the center of a proceeding—in the above example, the "ego" of the runner—is totally emptied, the proceeding itself—in this example, the run—comes to its greatest fullness. As soon as the center of the proceeding is no longer present, the proceeding is perfectly present. In this way emptiness and fullness, or nonpresence and presence, belong to each other and depend on one another. Perfect emptiness or nonpresence (of the runner) gives way to perfect fullness or presence (of the run).

In the *Daodejing*, the ruler is supposed to be at the center of the state, and he is required to empty himself in a fashion similar to the runner in the above example. The ruler's nonaction is expected to bring about the seamless functioning of the state—this is how he is supposed to "run" the state. In the *Zhuangzi*, the Daoist sage is supposed to forget his or her "ego" in every action. Thus, an action is complete when there is no interference from the ego. In the state, the nonpresence of the Daoist monarch, who manifests the empty center of the community, gives rise to the full presence of the state. When it comes to individual action, the nonpresence of the ego manifests the empty center of the action that gives rise to its full presence.

"Sitting in Forgetfulness" (*zuo wang*) is an expression for the practice of Daoist philosophy. This phrase (which can be found, for instance, in the *Zhuangzi*) designates a type of meditation which results in the "losing of the 'I'" (*sang wo*).[35] By losing one's ego, one empties the center of one's existence. In exactly this way one can transform one's existence into the ideal scenario of the Dao. One's life becomes an egoless but continuous and perfect run. The following images and allegories were designed to illustrate how this could be done.

Images and Allegories

1. Images in the *Daodejing*

THE WHEEL—AN IMAGE OF THE DAO

The eleventh chapter of the *Daodejing* begins with the following lines:

> Thirty spokes are united in one hub.
>> It is in its [space of] emptiness,
>> Where the usefulness of the cart is.

The image of the cart, or rather the image of the wheel that carries the cart along its way, is an image of the Dao. It offers access to the Daoist world of imagery and provides an orientation or a framework for understanding and connecting the various motifs and topics of this philosophy.

That the Dao is depicted as a wheel, as the wheel of a cart, shows right away that the Dao is not static, that it is not something that eternally stands still, but rather something that moves—even though it does not change its shape. The wheel is not merely a thing, it is also a kind of event, it is rotation and motion. The wheel is a running, it is a "pro-ceeding," a "pro-cess" (i.e., literally a "going-forwards"). Since the Dao is like a wheel, it is—for instance, unlike a rock (which is, as it is generally known, a quite important image in Christianity)—less a foundation or a principle for things or beings than a structure or a pattern of happenings. The image of the wheel demonstrates that the Dao is not to be understood as a divine source or a higher "form" in the Platonic sense. It is neither an ultimate origin or creator, nor a fundamental law of logic or nature. It is distinguished from such things (with which some Western interpreters sometimes confused it) by being an *instruction model* rather than a *cause*. By depicting the Dao as a wheel, the Daoists show not what something is based upon, but rather how something *goes*.

The image of the wheel shows how a mechanism or an organism has to be structured in order to function well. By analyzing the elements that constitute the wheel, one analyzes the elements that, according to ancient Daoism, are constituents of a perfect scenario of efficacy. The two basic elements of the wheel named in the first line of the eleventh chapter of the *Daodejing* are the spokes and the hub (the hole in which, when a cart is built, the axle is put). If one understands their respective functions and their relation to each other, one realizes what ancient Daoism saw as essential factors determining the success or failure of an action or a process.

At the center of the wheel there is the hub, just as at the center of any efficient scenario there has to be an empty middle. This element of the scenario has four main characteristics: it is positioned at the *center*, it is *empty*, it does not move and thus it is *still*, and, fourth and finally, being a center it is *single*.

All the spokes connect to the hub in the same way; none has a privileged position that would distinguish it from the other spokes. Only the hub has a special and a unique place within the wheel—it occupies the *center*.

The hub is not made of something. All the spokes are made of a material substance, whereas the hub is nothing but an empty space; it does not have any positive qualities. Because the material the spokes are made of is necessarily always a specific one, it is exchangeable. The wood of this or that tree can be used, one can even use something other than wood. No matter which material is used for making the spokes, the hub remains untouched. It is always made out of the same nonmaterial. Materials like wood grow and wither, metal is cast and rusts. An empty space neither withers nor rusts. It is either there or not; its emptiness cannot increase or diminish in substance. There are no degrees of emptiness. (We say, of course, that a glass is "half empty," but this is said in regard to the glass, not in regard to the emptiness—when we drink more, the glass becomes increasingly empty, that is, the emptiness covers more space, but it does not change substan-

tially—unlike the bourbon when we add ice.) All the spokes cannot but be material and therefore cannot but have a positive definition. The empty space lacks exactly this. If it was to be positively
defined, it would not be *empty*.

Whereas the spokes turn around within the wheel, the hub
always stands still. Unchanged, it keeps its position and it does this
simply by doing nothing. But this nonaction allows for the
"action" of the spokes: it allows them to turn around in a regular
and harmonious way. The stillness of the hub is the "source" for
the orderly movement of the spokes. The circular rotation requires
a pivot. Without such an unmoving central point, the movement
of the spokes will immediately lose its balance. The wheel will no
longer run smoothly and soon it will bend or break. The perfect
circular movement of the spokes is anchored in the stillness of the
hub. The continuous stability of the wheel is entirely dependant on
the hub's being incessantly *still*.

Many spokes are united in one hub. No matter how many
spokes a wheel actually has, it will always have only one hub. The
spokes are necessarily a multitude, the hub is necessarily single. In
the strict sense, a geometric middle within a circle is always one.
The hub is not only numerically one—it is also the place *uniting*
the spokes. All spokes "are united in one hub." In this way, the
hub provides for the unity of the wheel by being *single*.

Within a state, the Daoist regent is supposed to rule like the
hub within a wheel. The Daoist sage ruler should share the (negative) characteristics of the hub: centrality, emptiness, stillness, and
singularity. Being in the middle of the people, all turn towards the
ruler just like the spokes turn towards the hub. While the ruler is
one, he provides for the unity of all, being "al*one*," he makes "all
one":

> When the sage resides in the world,
>   he fuses himself with it.
> For the world he merges hearts.
> All the people fix ears and eyes on him,
>   and the sage regards them as smiling children.
>
> (*Daodejing* 49)

The ruler is the center of the kingdom; and everybody turns to
him in the same way. His subjects encircle him like the spokes

encircle a hub, and they rely on him to merge them together into a unit. He, however, calls himself the "orphaned" and the "abandoned" (*Daodejing* 39, 42). He is single and has no one to specifically relate to. To him, all are the same, but no one is of his kind. The ruler remains unmoved at his lonely position within the community. He never leaves his place and is aware of everything "without going" anywhere (*Daodejing* 47). He is "tranquil and still, in order to adjust the world" (*Daodejing* 45). The ruler's nonaction enables the subjects to fulfill their respective duties and tasks. Because he does not interfere and only keeps to his position, all do their jobs properly. The well-ordered community sees the ruler inactive and calm, while everybody surrounding him is actively engaged. All activities are merged into a unity by the ruler's immobility. He is not only free of action, but also of inclinations, intentions, or propensities. By being empty of any personal interests, he is ultimately "fair" and relates to everyone in the same way—again like a hub relates in the same way to all individual spokes.

The ruler's position within a state corresponds to the position of the hub within a wheel. Following the same pattern, the position of the "hub" or of the "ruler" in the human body is taken on by the heart, or *xin*—which was also supposed to be the center of mental activity and therefore is often translated as "heart-mind." The Sinologist Isabelle Robinet describes the likeness of the social and physical bodies with the following words: "The human body is also analogous to the organization of a nation, which was conceived as an organism throughout Chinese tradition. Many Daoist texts present this concept in a precise and developed way, relating each organ to an official, with the ruling organ, the heart, the homologue of the prince."[1] Like the hub and the sage ruler, the heart has to be *empty* and is not supposed to be stirred in any way. All activities have to be performed by the organs. The heart is at the center of all bodily functioning and it alone "rules"—it is the unifying element of the organism. Daoist practice reveres the so-called immortals (*xian*) who perfected their bodies in such a way that they have become an everlasting organic circulation of life energies. Around the empty heart—which is also empty of any emotions—the bodily functioning takes its steady and never-ending course.

The spokes are in a certain sense the opposite of the hub. While the hub is at the center, the spokes are in the *periphery*; while the hub is empty, the spokes are *full*; while the hub is still, the spokes are in *motion*; and while the hub is single, the spokes are *many*. In the state, the subjects—the people and the officials—correspond to the spokes, and in the physical body they are the organs. The spokes represent the realm of the visible and the realm of activity. They are the image for everything that has a definite and "positive" place—although these positions are constantly changing. When the wheel is turning, the spokes occupy every position: top and bottom, left and right. They run through the whole "positive" space of the wheel. Through their constant turning, they mark the space and the borders of activity. This space of activity or motion is itself a space of opposition: top and bottom, and left and right. The space created by the turning of the spokes is constructed by the exchanging of opposite positions. Within the process of rotation the spoke on top changes places with the spoke on the bottom, and so forth. The whole periphery performs a constant, harmonious alteration, a perfectly regular course of turnovers.

The spokes divide the wheel into different segments, into separate compartments. The division is such that none of the segments overlap. All the separate segments cover their own specific space at a specific time—and in the perfectly ordered community all the different professions are supposed to only perform their specific jobs at the right times. Any interference or blurring between realms would damage the harmonious division of activities. The spinning of the wheel is smooth as long as the spokes are kept apart from each other and do not overstep the boundaries they themselves have drawn. In the community, duties and hierarchies change in the course of time—a child who has to follow the lead of its parents grows into a parent who has to lead children. On the same stretch of land one sows in the spring and harvests in autumn. While continuous changes occur, there is always the danger of events getting out of order and becoming inefficient. When there is movement, there can be confusion, there can be delays, and there can be resistance. Therefore, it is of the utmost importance that a clear order continuously regulates what goes on. At all times tasks have to be distinctly divided so that they fit harmoniously with each other. The image of the wheel shows how distinct segments can seamlessly combine into an ideally working whole. If in society officials competed for mandates, if professionals intermingled in each other's works, or if the body's organs tried to take up each other's functions, then the state or the body would break down, just like a wheel whose spokes tried to occupy each other's space.

The order of the spokes within a wheel is based on the relation of opposite positions: top and bottom, left and right, and so forth. This opposition in the realm of the spokes is, however, only "relative," and not "absolute." First, the relation of the spokes to each other is not antagonistic, but complementary—they match. Second, the opposition is only momentary: the positions constantly change. The complementary opposition of the spokes within a running wheel resembles the natural cycle of time. In the course of the changes from day to night, from month to month, and from one season to the next, complementary segments follow each other in a cyclic sequence. In an agrarian society, people have to arrange their activities in accordance with the rhythm of time. The tasks of spring and autumn are in opposition to each other—in the spring one nourishes life, in the autumn one terminates it—but they complement each other, rounding up the year.

As opposed to the relative opposition in the realm of spokes, the opposition between the spokes and the hub may be called "absolute." The hub never changes places with any of the spokes, and a spoke is never allowed to occupy the central spot of the wheel. Likewise, in society the subjects will have to perform different tasks at different times, but they will never be charged with becoming the ruler. The ruler, too, can never be allowed to meddle with the activities of any of his subjects. If he would do so, he would, by leaving his position, endanger the well-being of the whole country. A wheel may still run when a spoke breaks, but if something happens to the hub, the whole wheel is disrupted.

Only from the perspective of the wheel as a whole is the opposition between the spokes and the hub evened out. In its rotation, the wheel in itself is a complementary unit of spokes and hub. The spokes and the wheel cannot be taken apart: If they are taken apart, the spokes cease to be spokes and the hub ceases to be a hub. If the wheel breaks, the spokes are only pieces of wood; and there would be no trace of the hub—it just disappears. Similarly, a ruler without a people is not a ruler. And if people are not united by a common government or social order, they do not form a union or comm-unity. In the body, the organs cannot exist without the heart, and the heart cannot exist without the organs.

Although the "absolute" opposite constituents of hub/spokes, ruler/people, and heart/organs never change their differing roles, they still form a single and indivisible unit. If they split apart, they both disappear.

The hub represents the inner unity of the wheel. It unites the spokes and is the pivot for all "contradictory" movement. In addition to the inner unity of the wheel, there is the greater unity of the moving wheel as a whole and as a process. Within the wheel, the hub is some sort of "leader"; it is the decisive and core element. Accordingly, the ruler is the "leader" of the state—albeit a leader without personal intentions or inclinations—and the heart "leads" the body. In this sense, the hub can be identified with the course of the whole wheel, just like a state is sometimes identified with its ruler or the body with the heart. The inner unity implies the greater unity of the whole. Even in everyday English it is quite common to identify a larger unit by its leading part. News reports inform us, for instance, about what "Washington" or "Ottawa" decided—meaning, of course, the American or Canadian government, and thus the United States or Canada as a whole nation. These are special cases of a *pars pro toto* figure of speech in which the central element is identified with the whole. It is important to note that the Daoists often use the term *Dao* in a similarly ambiguous fashion. It can, on the one hand, be a designation for the "inner unity" of a perfect scenario; it can, so to speak, be the "name" of the empty hub within the wheel. On the other hand, it can also connote the "greater unity" of the whole wheel and its continuous rotation. This double meaning is concisely summarized by a short statement about the Dao in the book *Guanzi*:

> Regarding its greatness, there is nothing beyond it.
> Regarding its smallness, there is nothing within it.[7]

Insofar as the Dao can be identified as the empty center or the hub, it contains nothing. Since there is nothing within it, it is the smallest of all things. But insofar as the Dao can also be identified with everything that is going on, or in the image of *Laozi* 11, with the whole wheel, there is nothing that does not take part in its movement. Being all-inclusive, the Dao is of the greatest extension. The Dao, as both the inner and greater unity of all perfect happenings, is nowhere and everywhere at the same time. It is both the hub and the wheel.

One has to be aware of this ambiguous meaning of the term Dao—as illustrated by the multifaceted image of the wheel—to better understand the many paradoxes that Daoist texts tend to play with. The best-known Daoist paradox—in various forms—is probably the famous maxim "doing nothing and nothing is undone" (*wu wei er wu bu wei*) as it is found in chapters 37 and 48 of the *Daodejing*. The image of the wheel demonstrates exactly this: how the inactive hub is the foundation of the perfect activity of the wheel. The Dao is both inactive and active, depending on which of its aspects one focuses on. If one looks at it "regarding its smallness," then it does nothing. If one looks at it "regarding its greatness," then nothing is undone.

So far, I have tried to analyze the image of the wheel in terms of its structure. But one can also look at it in other ways. There are several motifs or associations tied to this image. There are two eminent Daoist concepts that are intimately connected with the image of the wheel: "Permanence" (*chang, heng*) and the distinctive notion of "self-so" (*ziran*).

The end of the sixteenth chapter of the *Daodejing* equates being in accord with the Dao with "not being imperiled by bodily decay." The main Daoist indicator of efficacy or perfection is permanence. The more lasting an organism is, the more durable a scenario, the more it corresponds with the Dao. The perfect Daoist wheel runs incessantly. The Daoist vision of permanence is addressed in the very first sentence of the *Daodejing* (in the standard edition), and throughout the book it is applied to various cases. While passages like those in chapter 16 speak about the permanence of the body, many others speak about the permanence of the state, and some speak about the permanence of the cosmos: "Heaven is enduring, the earth is long-lasting" says chapter 7. The cosmic realms of heaven and earth constitute an environment of constancy for human beings. It is up to man to make human society equally stable and permanent.

Sinologists have frequently pointed out that the philosophically most fruitful period of ancient China—which was also the founding period of Daoism—was characterized by uninterrupted political, and very often military, conflict. In this age of the so-called Warring States (475–221 BCE), the central rule of the kings of

Zhou was only nominal because the many former imperial fief-
doms had in reality developed into independent states. These
political entities threatened each other's existence and every single
state more or less constantly faced the question of how to secure
its very existence. The Dao of the Daoists was one of the answers
to this question. In this context, the images of permanence in the
Daodejing served as material for lectures in political strategy.

When Daoist practitioners "took over" the *Daodejing*, the
images of permanence were interpreted in a more physical way. In
this context, the art of permanence was believed to primarily consist in the cultivation of the body, and special attention was given to
the unharmed and intact body. They attempted some kind of bodily closure in order to avoid any loss of energy. It was feared that the
body might "leak" life energy through the bodily openings and,
specifically, through activities of the senses—just like in the case of
the mythical figure of Hundun described in the *Zhuangzi*. Hundun
had a perfect and permanent life at the *center* of the world, but was
devoid of personal features—he had no face. The kings from the
periphery decided to come to the center and do Hundun a favor by
giving him a facial shape. They drilled seven holes into his body—
the facial openings—and he immediately perished.[3] Guo Xiang
comments laconically on this story: "*Activism ruined him.*"[4] The
legend of Hundun can easily be read along the structural lines of
the image of the wheel—when the periphery interferes with the
center and bereaves it of its vacuity, when there is action where nonaction should be, then durability is destroyed. But the drilling of
the holes also expresses the Daoist fear that openings may destroy a
perfect organism. Chapter 52 of the *Daodejing* says: "Fill the openings, close the entries—be unencumbered by the termination of the
body." The perfect organism is closed like a wheel. It runs without
friction or leak. Openings harm the ideal closure and endanger the
permanence of its functioning.

The ideal of permanence is accompanied by the ideal of the
"self-so" (*ziran*). The Daoist ever-turning wheel resembles a *perpetuum mobile*: Nothing starts it turning. The twenty-fifth chapter
of the *Daodejing* says: "The Dao follows the law of its 'own course'
[*ziran*]." The term *ziran* literally means "self-so." It is the "natural" or "spontaneous" way things and events take by themselves. It
is their "own course." The "self-so" or the "own course" of the
wheel corresponds to the nonaction of the hub in the midst of its

motion. The "ruling" element does not interfere, and therefore events do not depend on any initiative. They do not depend on any external impulse and so go on by themselves. If they were dependent on an external initiative or impulse, they would not be self-sufficient, and once the impulse was exhausted, events would soon come to an end. The Daoist heart, ruler, or hub are not "first movers" since they themselves do not move anything. The hub does not move the spokes, the spokes rather turn around the hub by themselves—they take their "own course" and run in a "self-so" way. When the ruler does not act, all the people will "spontaneously" do what has to be done, and they will say: "it happens to us 'self-so,'" as chapter 17 of the *Daodejing* puts it. The permanence of the perfect scenario is based on a sort of *autopoiesis* or self-generation. The closure of the mechanism keeps it independent from any external origin or input. The perfect mechanism includes its own source.

The image of the wheel is a fundamental image of the Dao, and there are many more Daoist images with similar structures.

WATER AND THE FEMALE

Water is an important symbol in many different traditions and cultures. Ancient Chinese philosophers made ample use of it—not only the Daoists, but also the Confucians and many others.[5] In Daoist texts, the image of water is brought into play in a complex manifold of ways. While the image of the wheel is of a nearly systematic clarity, the image of water gives rise to a host of closely related associations that merge with one another. Thus, the image of water is somewhat blurred. The symbolics of water in Daoist texts may be divided into four aspects: Water as the *flowing of the Dao*, as a *nourishing source*, as that which always takes on the *lowest position*, and as the *soft which overcomes the hard*.[6]

That the Dao flows is made clear in chapter 34 of the *Daodejing*:

> The Dao—
>> How it flows!
>> Left and right it can be.

The Dao is movement. It flows like a stream. Its motion is natural and spontaneous, there is no mover, no visible force that would "run" the water. Water naturally flows in all directions. There is also a political allusion here: the "left and right" of the ruler are the ministers and officials who serve the state. Flowing from the unmoving center of the state, the Dao spreads out over the whole nation.

As far as the image of the water stands for the flow of the Dao spreading out to cover all there is, there is also an association of shapelessness and endlessness connected to it. The stream becomes the sea. The Dao is "formless" just "like the ocean," says chapter 20 of the *Daodejing*. Water flows towards the sea and in the course of this journey it gets naturally larger and larger. It grows into a never-ending and unlimited amorphous ocean.

Other aspects of the Daoist imagery of water can be found in chapter 8 of the *Daodejing*:

> The best is like water.
>> The goodness of water consists in
>> its being beneficial to the ten thousand things,
>> and in that it, when there is contention, takes on the place
>> which the mass of the people detest.
> Thus [the best] is close to the Dao.
> Its position
>> is good in placement.
> Its heart
>> is good in depth.
> Its giving
>> is good in nature.

These lines of the *Daodejing* can once again be read as political advice. Seen in this manner, the Dao is the Dao of the government, and "the best" is the best ruler. The perfect regent is described by the virtues of water: He is "close to the Dao" because he is able to be "like water." Water is beneficial to all things and all people; it nourishes them and keeps them alive. This is exactly the duty of the ruler. He is supposed to be the source of the people's well-being. Not only is his duty like that of water, but also his strategy: Water always flows downwards and it occupies the lowest of places. The perfect ruler will follow this course and—as opposed to the masses—will take the place that no one else wants. He occupies the lowest, most hidden position and refuses all titles that would somehow elevate him. Chapter

39 of the *Daodejing* says: "Exactly therefore / lords and kings call themselves the 'orphaned,' the 'abandoned,' and the 'unpropertied.' / It is in this way that they root themselves in the low, isn't it?" This modesty is strategically motivated. The ruler chooses the lowest and most hidden position so that all power will be concentrated in him. A core Daoist tactic is to *gain by loss*. Who retreats the most will be the most qualified for being the hidden regent. This is the "spirit of the valley" (*Daodejing*, chapter 6): The deeper, the darker, and the more hidden (*xuan*), the more powerful. Chapter 61 of the *Daodejing* expresses this with the imagery of water:

> A large state is
>   low lying waters
>   the female of the world
>   the connection of the world.
> The female overcomes the male
>   by constant stillness.
> Because she is still
>   she is therefore fittingly underneath.

This chapter mixes the imagery of water with the equally important imagery of femininity. Just as water occupies the lower position, so does femininity—and this is certainly to be understood not only socially, but also sexually. The lower waters take in or "conceive" what comes down from the higher waters. In this way, what lies above—the male—looses its energy to what lies below. The female overcomes the male. This is the "female conduct" (*ci jie*) that is celebrated in Huang-Lao-Daoism and the *Four Classics of the Yellow Emperor*. The power of the low is shared by the valley—another Daoist image that combines associations of fluids and fertility—and, even more so, by the sea. The sea is not only shapeless and endless, it also perfectly exemplifies the "feminine conduct" of lying low. Chapter 66 of the *Daodejing* says:

> Rivers and oceans
>   are able to be king of hundreds of valleys
>   because they have the goodness to lie lower than those.
> Exactly therefore
> they are able to be king of hundreds of valleys.

Exactly therefore:
If the sage wishes to be above the people
    he has to place himself below them in words.
If he wishes to be at the front of the people
    he has to put his person behind.

Everything flows naturally or "self-so" to the ocean and the feminine. There is a propensity in all things to do this—like there is a propensity of the spokes to be turned towards the hub. The perfect ruler has to copy the strategy of water and the feminine. If he does so, he can, in turn, be as beneficial as these and nourish all things. Like water and the feminine, the ideal ruler is supposed to naturally "conceive" all energy around him and thus be the source of life. Water and femininity are at the *center* of the circle of pro-creation. They are the "gate"—to use another Daoist image—of life, the empty center into which life enters and from which it comes forth.[7] The lowest waters and the feminine womb are the "low places" to which the fluids of life flow and from which life emerges. Chapter 32 of the *Daodejing* says: "In comparison, the Dao is to the world / what rivers and oceans are to small valleys."

The images of water and femininity, similar to the image of the wheel, illustrate a paradox: the weak will defeat the strong. All these images are therefore also images of the way to triumph. Chapter 78 of the *Daodejing* expresses this in all clarity:

Nothing in the world
    is smoother and softer than water,
but nothing is better than it
    in attacking the solid and strong—
because there is nothing to change it.

That the water defeats the massive,
that the soft defeats the hard—
    no one in the world who does not know this,
    but no one who knows to apply it.

Therefore the words of the sage are:
To take on the shameful in the state,
    this is to be lord of the altars of earth and grain.
To take on the unfavorable in the state,
    this is to be king of the world.

Right words are like the reverse.

"Right words are like the reverse"—the strategies of water and femininity are paradoxical, but they are strategies of the Dao. This is to say that they are "natural" strategies, and thus strategies that, from a Daoist perspective, cannot fail. The symbolics of water and femininity include the imagery of the "soft"—which overcomes the hard. The image of softness connects to images of adaptability and flexibility, and both these characteristics are ascribed to water and the feminine. Once again, these images have certainly also a sexual and physical aspect to them for it is said that "the soft defeats the hard." All of these symbols and images are connected, and they also connect to the imagery of the wheel.

THE ROOT

Another important Daoist image that relates to the symbolics associated with the wheel, water, and femininity is the image of the root (Chinese: *ben* or *gen*). This image has been especially influential in a line of interpretation of Daoist philosophy that goes back to Wang Bi.[8] In this context, the image of the root can be understood as a symbol of the Dao as a "transcendent" origin of the world or cosmos. Such an interpretation, however, goes far beyond the actual use of this image in ancient Daoist texts, such as the *Daodejing* and the *Zhuangzi*. The image of the root, I believe, should rather be understood in analogy and in direct correlation to the other images within these texts, such as those described above. The image of the root certainly portrays the Dao as some kind of "origin," but not as a divine creative force. It rather shows that Daoist philosophy conceived of "creation" as something without an absolute beginning, it is an on-going process of which its origin is an *integral* part. The "origin" is not beyond or next to what is originated, it is rather always within that which is, and has no place outside of this. The image of the root is, so to speak, an image of an *autopoietic* (self-generating) or "acosmotic"[9] worldview.

Wang Bi makes use of the image of the root in his commentary on chapter 40 of the *Daodejing*. This short chapter states:

> Reversal is the movement of the Dao.
> Weakness is the usefulness of the Dao.
>
> The things of the world are brought to life by presence.
> Presence is brought to life by nonpresence.

Wang Bi mentions the "root" two times in his explanations of this philosophical saying. In his commentary he writes:

> The high has the low as its fundament. The appreciated has the depreciated as its root. [. . .] All the things in the world come into life by presence. Presence takes its beginning in nonpresence as its root.

The root is indeed introduced here as something fundamental. One may conclude from Wang's commentary that it is supposed to represent a kind of *arche* or ultimate starting point. The root stands for the Dao and for nonpresence or emptiness (*wu*), and here it might also stand for a first beginning. If so, Wang Bi would be saying quite the opposite of the *Zhuangzi*—as will be discussed later in this book in the section on time. The *Zhuangzi* points out the futility of a philosophical search for an ultimate beginning. All that is originated is part of a process of origination, but there is no origination at the origin of origination.

The root does not exist *before* the rest of the plant. It is a part of the plant, albeit a special one. The root is where growth originates, but it is nevertheless totally integrated with the rest of the plant (like the hub is totally integrated with the rest of the wheel). The root is not something *metaphysical* with respect to the plant, it does in no way transcend the plant's physical existence. The root is at the same time the origin of the growth of the plant and a physical part of it. To be sure, the root is different from the visible parts of the plant. It is invisible (like the empty hub) and in a certain sense the source of the plant—but it is never something separate. In this way the root illustrates the Daoist concept of self-generation or *autopoiesis*, a concept that is quite the contrary of a concept of external causation, for instance by an omnipotent creator or God.

In chapter 6 of the *Daodejing*, the image of the root appears together with the images of water and femininity (and with the image of the gate):

> The spirit of valley does not die—
> This is called: dark femininity.
> The gate of dark femininity—
> This is called: root of heaven and earth.

How on-going!
    As it were existent.
    In its use inexhaustible.

In this chapter, the image of the water is "hidden" in the image of the valley—which derives its fertility from the stream running through it. The lowest place is the place that provides the heights around it with life. These images are accompanied in this chapter by the image of the root. The root is also "dark," it is hidden under the surface, and it is the lowest part of the plant. It is, by these characteristics, the source of nourishment for the plant. By virtue of its low position it is able to "conceive" all energy and, in return, to give life. In this fashion, the Dao is the "root of heaven and earth." The text explicitly states that this root is "as it were existent." The root is nonpresent, it is permanently out of sight, but it is still "there," it is always "with" the present and visible parts of the plant. The nonpresent origin is nevertheless somehow existent. It is an origin that is always tied to the originated.

The root is hidden in the dark, but it is (like the hub) at the center of the process that it originates. While the plant blossoms and withers, the root stays unmoved and unchanged. It never leaves its position during the plant's life cycle. It is the gate of fertility through which the plant emerges and into which it recedes. The plant's life is concentrated on and balanced by the root, just as the spokes are concentrated on and balanced by the hub. The root is still and quiet, tranquil and motionless. It is the permanent center of the permanent change in the visible realm of the impermanent. One has to know about this "natural" structure of permanence and change, of fertility and success, in order to be a Daoist expert in the art of government. The images of the *Daodejing* are supposed to teach this knowledge and skill.

The root is deeply hidden in the dark and it possesses all the nourishing energies. It never exhausts itself by blossoming—it does not expose itself to the frictions of a life in the realm of the visible present. It accommodates itself to the earth around it and thus can be perfectly *sparing*. By being sparing it is spared from withering. The root practices the strategies of "self-so" generation and preservation, and images of this are combined and connected to the Daoist art of government in chapter 59 of the *Daodejing*:

For ruling men,
for serving heaven,
    nothing compares to being sparing.
Well, by being sparing alone,
    early accommodation comes about.
Early accommodation is called:
    multiple accumulation of power [*de*]—
    so that nothing is not overcome.
He by whom nothing is not overcome—
    no one knows his end.
Because no one knows his end
    he can possess the state.
Because he possesses the mother of the state,
    he can last long.
This is called: being deep-rooted and firmly based.
This is the Way of long life and lasting vision.

This chapter blends together the Daoist imagery that has been discussed so far. The perfect exercise of power is called "deep-rooted" and compared to "possessing the mother of the state." The Daoist art of government is a method described as soft and feminine. And this method is supposed to bring about a perfect and enduring scenario of productivity structured by an empty, nonpresent center and a present, ever-changing periphery.

2. Allegories from the *Zhuangzi*

The images of the *Daodejing* form a tightly interwoven symbolic network. This network of images and symbols, however, is not developed into a stringent philosophical "plot." The 81 chapters of the *Daodejing* are an assembly of raw poetic materials that leave the construction of a philosophical narrative to the reader. This is quite different than the *Zhuangzi*, which is closer in style to what may be called philosophical prose. It contains numerous allegories that, if one takes a close look at them, can be read as highly aesthetic expressions of a complex philosophical story. The philosophical structures and patterns that shape the images of the *Daodejing* come to new life in the *Zhuangzi*. Here, the philosophical lore of the *Daodejing* is transformed into a more refined and shrewd work of art.

THE DREAM OF THE BUTTERFLY—OR: EVERYTHING IS REAL

Herbert A. Giles's translation of the famous allegory of the butterfly dream in the *Zhuangzi* is beautiful, but unfortunately, as I believe, entirely wrong:

> Once upon a time, I, Zhuangzi, dreamt I was a butterfly, fluttering hither and thither, to all intents and purposes a butterfly. I was conscious only of following my fancies as a butterfly, and was unconscious of my individuality as a man. Suddenly, I awaked, and there I lay, myself again. Now I do not know whether I was then a man dreaming I was a butterfly, or whether I am now a butterfly, dreaming I am a man. Between a man and a butterfly there is necessarily a barrier. The transition is called *Metempsychosis.*[10]

I quote this translation because of its great influence on the Western perception of Daoist philosophy, especially—as pointed out in the introduction—among Western intellectuals and philosophers. Giles's translation of the *Zhuangzi* and, in particular, his rendering of this allegory is representative of the general understanding of Daoist philosophy in his generation while, on the other hand, it quite obviously contradicts a traditional interpretation of the text in China.

Giles's translation of the butterfly dream has little to do with the original. It is rather an interesting transformation of the text into the patterns of "standard" Western philosophy. Perhaps the butterfly allegory became so popular in the West just because of this "Westernization." When one first reads Giles's version, it surely sounds very Chinese—if only because of the Chinese names and the quite "oriental" butterfly. But upon taking a closer look, it turns out to be an exotic disguise of thoroughly Western ideas. Giles's translation can be compared to the food of many Chinese restaurants in Western countries: it looks Chinese, but the cook has, nevertheless, made it wonderfully palatable to eaters accustomed to the local tastes.

Giles's version is based on Zhuangzi's recollection of his dream after he wakes up. Philosophically speaking, the story revolves around a central act of consciousness. Once the philosopher awakes, he remembers his dream of the butterfly, and once he starts remembering this dream, he begins to doubt and to reflect on his being and on the problems of truth and appearance. In

Giles's rendering, Zhuangzi gains an insight into the continuity of the soul within the chain of existence: he understands that he is part of the great cycle of *Metempsychosis* or the transmigration of the soul. The act of remembering is at the core of this philosophical realization of the truth. It seems to be the point of departure on the path towards the discovery of the truth about the world and one's soul.

Giles's butterfly dream story is an interesting blend of motifs from the Western philosophical tradition. It bears a certain resemblance to the final book of Plato's *Republic* in which Socrates tells the myth of Er, a person who was allowed to visit the underworld. In the underworld, Er witnessed what happens to the souls there: after their lives on earth, they are judged and sent either to a heaven or to a hell. Having spent a certain amount of time in the underworld, the souls return to earth after choosing a new body for their next life. Before the souls re-enter the world, they have to cross the plains of *Lethe*—or: Forgetfulness. By this crossing, they lose all their memory of the underworld and go on to live without knowledge of the *metempsychosis* they have undergone. According to this story, it is only through the act of remembrance—through mentally reaching back before the plains of forgetfulness—that human beings can actually realize their true being and fate: the transmigration of souls.

Since Plato, *remembrance* has been a central motif within Western conceptions of wisdom and knowledge, of thinking and of truth. In Plato's *Meno*, Socrates tries to prove that all knowledge comes from memory by conducting an "experiment" with an uneducated slave: Just by asking the slave simple yes-or-no questions, Socrates helps him "discover" some basic geometrical rules. He concludes that the slave already had an innate geometrical knowledge and only needed some help to actually remember it. In modern philosophy, G. W. F. Hegel depicted recollection as the way that leads to absolute knowledge in the course of his *Phenomenology of Spirit*.[11] Old-European philosophers indeed often "thought back" to find the truth. In a similar way, Herbert A. Giles's Zhuangzi has to think back and re-member his dream in order to have the re-flection which leads him to re-cognize what is true and what only seems to be.

A second core motif of Giles's butterfly dream story deeply rooted in the Western philosophical tradition is expressed by the most often used term in his translation: *I*. This I and the related question of what this I truly *is* make up the philosophical thread that runs through the story. Zhuangzi tells a story about himself, he tells how his I in his dream is the I of a butterfly. Then he awakes and Zhuangzi is, as he says, "*myself* again." This very I then starts thinking—and what does it think about? About itself and about what it is! Giles's text is from beginning to end about the I and its reflection on its own being. It is an ironic fact, I believe, that in the history of Western philosophy, there are few texts that treat so exclusively and comprehensively the issue of human subjectivity!

A third core motif of Giles's butterfly dream story is *doubt*. As soon as Zhuangzi remembers his dream, he begins doubting. And again, these doubts are rather existential since they are in regard to his inner self. Did Zhuangzi dream about being a butterfly or is he now a butterfly dreaming he is Zhuangzi? The motif of philosophical doubt is of great importance within the history of Western philosophy. Although Rene Descartes' famous *Meditations* are usually summarized by the "motto" *cogito ergo sum* or "I think, therefore I am," one might as well use the motto "I doubt, therefore I am." At least after Descartes, Western philosophers are often seen as experts in doubting, as depicted in Auguste Rodin's sculpture *The Thinker*. The tradition of Western philosophy has combined these three motifs—remembrance, the being of the "I," and doubt—in various ways. One could very well write a history of (modern) Western philosophy by following the development of these notions. In Giles's translation, Zhuangzi appears to be a paradigmatic Western philosopher in an ancient Chinese robe!

A fourth Old-European motif which appears in Giles's butterfly dream comes into play at the end of the story: the motif of the *transition of a barrier* or *transcendence*. Once Zhuangzi has realized that there is a border between man and butterfly, he also realizes that he himself as a philosopher can have knowledge of this border and thus that he can philosophically go beyond it. Zhuangzi, by his reflection, can overstep the border between dreaming and being awake, between appearance and truth. This motif alludes to the Western—and especially Judaeo-Christian—distinction between immanence and transcendence. A "meditating" philosopher in the West can mentally reach beyond the barriers of this-worldly immanence and its merely apparent reality.

In this way, he or she can move to the higher realm of an infinite, divine, and true world, just like the freed prisoner in Plato's allegory of the cave.

A fifth Old-European motif in Giles's butterfly dream is closely connected to the previous one—it is the motif of the unreality or at least the *relativity of the world of experience*. From the perspective of the "awakened" philosopher, Zhuangzi sees through the unreality of his dreams. What he believed to be true while he was asleep, his then this-worldy and temporally limited existence as a butterfly, is finally unmasked as mere appearance, as a realm of only partial reality. Once the barrier is overcome, then what only seemed to be true is seen as it is. The awakened philosopher looks down on his earlier "unenlightened" experience. Only his mental reflection can elevate him to the realm of truth and free himself from the illusions of dreamlike sensual and temporal experience. In Giles's version, Zhuangzi seems to live through the process of a philosophical transition from the dreamlike phenomenal world to the enlightened realm of the noumenal.

The most wonderful transformation of the butterfly dream is, in my view, not the one of Zhuangzi in the story, but rather those performed by Herbert A. Giles. Giles's rendering keeps the oriental surface of the story alive, but completely converts the philosophical content into motifs of the Western philosophical tradition. Giles's magical transformation of the story has been overlooked by many of its Western readers who do not have access to the original texts. If one, however, takes a look at what the text literally says (or rather at what it does *not* say), and at how its ancient Chinese editor Guo Xiang (252–312) explains its meaning, one will see no evidence of the five motifs discussed above. In the Chinese original, the decisive turning point of the story is not remembering but *forgetting*. And this forgetting also includes the I and its being—it turns out that there is literally *no I and no being* in the story. Where Giles introduced doubts in the story, there is *doubtlessness* in the original, and where he advises the philosopher to transcend barriers, the original advises one to *accept borders*. Finally, while Giles's story seems to indicate the relativity of the dream world of temporal phenomena, the original text highlights the *equivalent reality of all experience*. If one reads the butterfly dream story along with Guo Xiang's commentary, one sees the text in a Daoist light.

The crucial difference between the plot of this allegory in Giles's translation and in Guo Xiang's edition is Zhuangzi's reaction when he awakes from his dream. While Giles implies that Zhuangzi remembers his dream, no such remembrance is mentioned in the text, and Guo Xiang's commentary makes it perfectly clear that Zhuangzi does *not* remember the dream—he has, rather, completely forgotten it. Once Zhuangzi—or as he is called in the story: Zhuang Zhou—awakes, Guo Xiang inserts the following commentary:

> Now Zhuang Zhou is just as ignorant about the butterfly as the butterfly was ignorant about Zhuang Zhou during the dream.[12]

When Zhuang Zhou awakes, he is as unaware of his earlier dream existence as the butterfly in the dream was unaware of Zhuang Zhou's earlier waking existence. Since the plot is completely different, the story has to be read in another manner. This being so, I present my own translation based on the Chinese original and Guo Xiang's commentary:

> Once Zhuang Zhou dreamt—and then he was a butterfly, a fluttering butterfly, self-content and in accord with its intentions. The butterfly did not know about Zhou. Suddenly it awoke—and then it was fully and completely Zhou. One does not know whether there is a Zhou becoming a butterfly in a dream or whether there is a butterfly becoming a Zhou in a dream. There is a Zhou and there is a butterfly, so there is necessarily a distinction between them. This is called: the changing of things.[13]

As opposed to Giles's translation, the original is based upon the mutual ignorance of Zhuang Zhou and the butterfly. The text indicates that because of this mutual ignorance, because of the forgetting of previous dreams while being awake and because of the forgetting of previous periods of being awake while dreaming, there are no grounds for devaluating one phase of existence. Both phases are equally authentic or real because each does not remember the other. Because the butterfly does not know about Zhou, it is "self-content." Because Zhou does not remember his dream he is "fully and completely Zhou"—and without any doubts! Since Zhou and the butterfly do *not* remember each other, because the barrier between them is *not* crossed, the change between them is seamless, spontaneous, and natural! The harmonious "changing of things" is dependent upon the acceptance of the distinction and *not* on its transcendence.

In the original version of the text the core philosophical motif of the allegory is not remembering but forgetting. Zhuang Zhou's "state of consciousness" is not one of reflection or theoretical reasoning, but rather one of a man who has been emptied of mental reflection.

It is quite noteworthy that the word that most frequently occurs in Giles's rendering—the "I," which is used *ten* times in those few lines, without counting words like "my" and "myself"—does not appear in the original! With this "I," Giles has Zhuang Zhou narrate the story—which is simply wrong, because it is not told from this perspective. Moreover, the "I" becomes, against textual evidence, the necessary subject of the act of remembrance. In Giles's story Zhuang Zhou becomes "myself again"—there is nothing like this in the Chinese text.

While Zhuang Zhou emerges as the "subject" of change in Giles's version—he is first a man, then a butterfly, and then once more a man, there is *no continuous subject* mentioned in the text. The original text rather implies that instead of an "I" and its "individuality," which undergo change (another invention by Giles), there is a kind of "autonomy" for both the butterfly and Zhuang Zhou. There is, strictly speaking, no substantial "I" that is first awake, then asleep, and then awake again. It is exactly because there is no such single, individual—which literally means *in-divis-ible*—I connecting them that both the butterfly and Zhuang Zhou can each be so fully real. They are real because they are divisible, not because they are in-divisible! During the dream, the butterfly is fully the butterfly, and when awake, Zhuang Zhou is fully Zhou. In the original text the change is complete: In one's dream one turns into another full reality and thus one is no longer what one was before. One is no longer "oneself" when change takes place. Change turns one I into another. While in Giles's story there is *one* I that takes on different bodies (like the soul in the course of *metempsychosis*), there are *three* phases in the original text, first Zhuang Zhou awake, then the butterfly in the dream, and then, strictly speaking, another Zhuang Zhou after the dream. There is no continuous I that acts as a bridge between these three phases. This is the reason that all three stages can be equally real.

The third motif in Giles's story, the moment of doubt, also has no equivalent in the Chinese text. Since Zhuang Zhou does not remember his dream, he is totally ignorant about the existence of the butterfly, and so has no reason to doubt his existence. Once awake, Zhuang Zhou is, as the text says, "fully and completely" Zhuang Zhou and does not seem to doubt this fact by asking himself strange philosophical questions. He is not "thinking back," but rather as solidly assured of himself as the butterfly was of itself in the dream. Unlike Giles's version ("Now I do not know whether . . ."), there is no question raised by Zhuang Zhou in the original. In its place the conclusion is made by a "neutral" observer: Given the fact that the butterfly during the dream is as assured of its existence as Zhuang Zhou is of his reality when he is awake, there is no hierarchy of reality for an external observer. There is a reality to the perspective of each phase, so the neutral perspective cannot say that one phase is more authentic than another or that the butterfly is *merely* a dream. This being so, there can be *no doubt* that both phases, dreaming and being awake, are in-differently valid. Both phases are indifferent to each other and thus are not differently real. Both phases prove each other's reality. In the Chinese text the reader is left with no doubt about this.

The fourth motif in Giles's story finds its reverse in the original Chinese text. Here, it is not the crossing of boundaries that gives rise to "true" reality, but rather the affirmation and acceptance of them. Only if the one who is awake does not "think back" to his or her dreams and only if the dreamer does not "think back" to what he or she was when awake, can they both be "fully real." If, in a dream, one knew that it was a dream, one's dream would no longer be experienced as real. There is no word for "transition" in the Chinese text at all! It is an addition by the translator, just as the ten "I"s are! The reality of both states are dependant on *not* transgressing the borders of their segments of existence. Just as one is no longer really asleep when one realizes that one is dreaming, one is no longer really awake when one starts "living in a dream world." If one revitalizes earlier phases, for instance by way of recollection, one cannot but give up one's presence, which diminishes the fullness of the "here and now." Total presence and the authenticity of the here and now is necessarily based on the nonviolation of "natural" barriers. Transitions of these barriers will not bring about a higher reality but, on the contrary, take away from reality.

As the text says, the changing of things goes along *necessarily* with distinctions. The Chinese character for "distinction" contains as its main semantic element the character for "knife." Clear-cut distinctions and divisibility guarantee well-proportioned change. It is dangerous to disregard them.

In his commentary, Guo Xiang interprets the butterfly story as an allegory about life and death. Guo Xiang explains that just as one should not see dreaming as less real than being awake, one should not see death as less real than life. According to Guo Xiang, life and death are two equally valid phases of being or segments of change. This being so, one should not be anxious about death. If one just lives while being alive without worrying about death, then one can be as "fully and completely" alive as Zhuang Zhou was awake when he did not worry about his dreams. Likewise, when dead, one will not remember life, and therefore the dead can be as self-content and pleased as the butterfly was during the dream. Guo Xiang writes:

> Well, the course of time does not stop for a moment, and today does not persist in what follows. Thus yesterday's dream changes into a today. How could it be different with the change between life and death!? Why should one let one's heart be made heavy by being moved back and forth between them? Being one, there is no knowledge of the other. Being a butterfly while dreaming is genuine. Relating this to human beings: when alive one does not know whether one may later actually have beautiful concubines. Only the stupid think they really know that life is something delightful and death is something to be sad about. That is what is called "never having heard of the changing of things."[14]

It seems that Herbert A. Giles had not "heard of the changing of things." In his version of the story the reader is left with the nonauthenticity of dreams and asked to be ready for a transition of the immanence of life and death. This is not what the ancient Daoist Guo Xiang believed. To him, life and death were equally genuine and no realm of experience was to be devaluated. This contradicts the fifth motif of Giles's version of the story.

From a Daoist point of view, the change of something into its opposite is the condition for complete, seamless, and permanent change in general. It is decisive that there are no "bridges of recollection" in this process connecting the phases of change so that each phase can be fully present. This concept of change is illustrated quite drastically by another Daoist parable found in the *Huainanzi*. This story parallels the butterfly dream, and it goes like this:

> Once Duke Niuai was suffering from the illness of change. After seven days the change took place and he turned into a tiger. When his elder brother who looked after him came into his chamber to cover the corpse, the tiger caught the elder brother and killed him. A cultivated person had become a predator, claws and teeth transformed. Emotions and the heart had changed. Spirit and form had changed. The one who is now a tiger knows nothing about the one who earlier was a man. And the one who earlier was a man knew nothing about the one who now is a tiger. The two have replaced each other and changed into an opposite. Both were enjoying completeness of form.[15]

The transformation of Duke Niuai into a tiger corresponds to Zhuang Zhou's transformation into a butterfly. In both transformations there is total mutual ignorance of the respective phases of existence. Just as the butterfly and Zhuang Zhou were totally ignorant of each other, so too are Duke Niuai and the tiger. This ignorance marks the barrier between the segments of change that is not to be transgressed. Only in this way can all phases enjoy their respective "completeness of form." The opposite nature of human beings and tigers highlights this idea: As a man, Duke Niuai is cultivated, while the tiger, as a predator, is wild. The transformation is total, it includes the "emotions and the heart," and "spirit and form." The phases of change oppose each other like day and night, and therefore they perfectly complement one another and establish an ongoing process. The butterfly dream allegory and the parable of Duke Niuai's "illness of change" both illustrate how an incessant process of change entails complete "forgetfulness." Both stories ask the reader to accept the completeness of change in which there is no continuous "transmigrating" substance.

The allegory of the butterfly dream is not about *metempsychosis*, it is about the Daoist teaching of change. However, if a core element of this Daoist teaching is to forget about previous and future phases of change in order to fully exhaust the authenticity of the *one* present phase—why does the butterfly dream allegory (as well as the story of Duke Niuai) cover *several* phases of change? Who

can actually tell these stories? What is the perspective of the narrator if neither Zhuang Zhou nor the butterfly have the slightest
knowledge of each other? Giles "solved" this problem by inventing the "I" that is not in the Chinese original—and thereby completely transformed the story. In order to correctly answer this
important question one has to take a closer look at the first sentence of the original text and the particular way personal names are
used in the allegory.

The butterfly allegory (as well as the story of Duke Niuai)
begins with the word "once" (*xi*). If the story is told from the perspective of a narrator, this narrator obviously talks about events
that happened in the past. The personal names used in the story
indicate a similar time relation between the narrator and the plot:
The text is supposedly written by Zhuang-*zi*, that is by *Master*
Zhuang, the honorific designation of someone who has became a
sage.[16] This designation indicates a change in personality—it indicates that someone has changed into someone else. Master
Zhuang tells a story about Zhuang Zhou,[17] about a person that
was alive before there was Master Zhuang. Zhuang Zhou changed
into Master Zhuang, and Master Zhuang tells us a story about
events that happened when *once* there was a Zhuang Zhou. Master
Zhuang tells the story about a "Zhou" whom he no longer identifies with. The story is told from the perspective of someone who
is neither Zhuang Zhou nor the butterfly, but who is equally
"close" to both. From the perspective of the narrator there is no
difference in reality or authenticity between the butterfly and
Zhuang Zhou. Before there was Master Zhuang, there once was a
Zhuang Zhou, and there once was a butterfly. *Now*, when the
story is told by Master Zhuang, he is no longer either of the two.
The story is told by someone who does not identify with either
Zhuang Zhou or the butterfly, but who affirms both equally.

The perspective of Zhuang *zi* or *Master* Zhuang, the narrator,
is the perspective of the Daoist sage. The Daoist sage is in the
midst of Zhuang Zhou and the butterfly, in the midst of dreaming
and being awake, in the midst of life and death. Zhuangzi's perspective is, so to speak, the "zero-perspective." He tells the story
out of the empty center of the process of change, out of the axis
or the "pivot of Dao" (*dao shu*) as the same chapter of the
Zhuangzi puts it.[18] The Daoist sage dwells unchanged at the center of the process of change. The story is told from this neutral and

empty position, not from the position of a continuous I that undergoes change. It is told from the perspective of Zhuangzi, not from the perspective of either Zhuang Zhou or the butterfly.

The narrator of the butterfly dream story is a Daoist sage, and this sage, at the "pivot of the Dao" occupies the same position as the hub within a wheel. The butterfly dream allegory in the *Zhuangzi* is structured parallel to the image of the wheel in chapter 11 of the *Daodejing*. The image and the allegory both illustrate a perfect process of change. The spokes of the wheel, switching positions in the course of time, correspond to Zhuang Zhou and the butterfly. Just as what is on top changes into what is below, so a Zhuang Zhou changes into a butterfly, a dreamer turns into someone awake, and a Duke Niuai turns into a tiger. Within the process of change each phase is always *distinct*. The process runs smoothly as long as there is no transgression of barriers, as long as everything does not transcend its respective presence.

To the sage at the center of the process of change the segments of change are not only "relatively" authentic—each is fully and completely real. The position of the sage does not introduce a sort of "relativism"; it rather guarantees the full authenticity and completeness of the process of change. Master Zhuang does not take anything away from the reality of either Zhuang Zhou or the butterfly for he affirms and founds their complete reality. Likewise, the Daoist sage does not represent an insight into the "relativity" of life and death, but rather the affirmation of their complete reality. With the Daoist sage, life and death come to their equal and full authenticity.

The butterfly dream allegory speaks to both the sage and the nonsage: For those who are not sages, it is appropriate to be fully content with one's reality—to be fully alive without doubting one's "being" or reflecting on one's I. If one is fully awake while being awake and fully asleep while being asleep, one will always be fully present. Like in a political or physical organism, one should just naturally live up to one's position within an ongoing process.

If one has become a sage (and the Buddhists will later call this step the attaining of "enlightenment" or *wu*), if one is no longer either asleep or awake, either alive or dead, one has lost all identifications. One is then equally close to all phases, but never present in any, and nonpresent in the midst of a changing presence. From the zero-perspective one observes the spinning of the circle—like

Zhuangzi observes the change from Zhuang Zhou to the butterfly. While everything else is what it is, the sage lets it be. In this way the sage can be identified with the whole process of change, just as the hub can be identified with the whole wheel, or the heart with the whole body, or the sage ruler with the whole state. In the midst of changes, the sage is no longer a distinct phase, but the core of the whole process of *Dao*.

THE FISHNET ALLEGORY—OR: HOW TO FORGET THINKING

There is another famous allegory in the *Zhuangzi* that has been interpreted in a rather Western manner on the basis of its standard English translation. This story can also be understood quite differently if one looks at it from a "classical" Daoist perspective. Here is, first of all, the fishnet allegory of the *Zhuangzi* in Burton Watson's "standard" translation:

> The fish trap exists because of the fish; once you've gotten the fish, you can forget the trap. The rabbit snare exists because of the rabbit; once you've gotten the rabbit, you can forget the snare. Words exist because of meaning; once you've gotten the meaning, you can forget the words. Where can I find a man who has forgotten words so I can have a word with him?[19]

At first sight, this allegory seems to be easy to understand. Just as one uses certain tools for fishing and hunting in order to get what is desired but hard to catch, so too does human communication makes use of words in order to catch certain difficult ideas or meanings. And just as one no longer cares about the hunting tool once they have performed their job, one also no longer cares about linguistic tools once they conveyed a certain meaning or sense. Or in other words, with respect to the object and not to the tool: What matters is getting it and having it in one's hands. Just as what matters in fishing and hunting is getting the fish and the game, what matters with words is getting the idea or the meaning.

This does not sound terribly unfamiliar to Western philosophical ears, and today the fishnet allegory is usually interpreted in just this manner. It is said that what is essential for Daoism is the deeper meaning behind the texts or the words of the masters. Just as one may forget the fish trap once the fish is caught, one may also forget the Daoist texts and words once one has understood their true message. In respect to language, the words are consequently unimportant, for all that really counts are the "ideas." Expressed in formal terminology, the Daoist teaching would accordingly be: signifiers are arbitrary and negligible, all that really matters is the signified.

Such a reading of the fishnet allegory is similar to Giles's rendering of the butterfly dream story in that it strongly parallels "classical" Old-European philosophy. The concept that words are expressions of mental contents, which are representations of facts, can be traced back to at least Aristotle's *De Interpretatione*.[20] In order to understand facts, one must accordingly go beyond words to grasp the ideas that stand for the facts. Once one leaves words behind and arrives at the thoughts, one will comprehend the truth. In order to arrive at truth one has to arrive at ideas.

Readings of the fishnet allegory that focus on the "getting" of true ideas can be found not only in modern Western studies of Daoist thought, but also within the Chinese tradition. One example is Wang Bi, the above mentioned somewhat "metaphysical" commentator on the *Daodejing*.[21] I believe, however, that a close look at the text of the fishnet allegory, at Guo Xiang's commentary to it, and at the *Zhuangzi* and other ancient Daoist texts reveals that early Daoists wanted to say something very different with this parable, for the standard translation and interpretation miss a most decisive pun.

The decisive pun in the fishnet allegory is "hidden" in the two Chinese characters that in Watson's translation have been rendered as "[once you've] gotten the meaning." These two characters are in Chinese *de yi*, which literally means "to get (*de*) the meaning (*yi*)." The character for "meaning" can also be translated as "idea," "intention," "desire," or "wish." Thus it can both designate an unspecific mental content (as in "meaning" or "idea") as well as, more specifically, the "wish" or "desire" one has in mind. In the phrase *de yi*, the word *yi* is more often understood in the second sense of "desire" or "wish," so that the expression usually means (as in Mathews's Chinese-English Dictionary)[22] "to get one's desires." In this sense it often just means "to be satisfied" (as in the phrase *de yi de hen*, "exceedingly well satisfied"; see Mathews's Chinese-English Dictionary[23]). It is in this very sense that the phrase is used—with a slight grammatical variation—in its only other occurrence in the *Zhuangzi*.[24] One has to have this ambiguity in mind—that the phrase *de yi* literally means "to get the meaning" but is usually used in the sense of "to get one's desires" or simply "to be satisfied"—in order to fully understand the point of the fishnet allegory.

The philosophical point of the fishnet allegory is, I firmly believe, not at all merely that one is supposed to "forget words" in order to grasp the true meaning or idea of the Dao—as the standard "Aristotelian" interpretation maintains. It is rather, that to "get the meaning" or "idea" of the Dao means "to be satisfied"— and that this satisfaction consists in having nothing in one's mind, in having no specific "meanings" or "ideas." Thus, I will argue, that "to get the meaning" (*de yi*) in a Daoist sense means, paradoxically, to be perfectly content (*de yi*) by no longer having any mental contents.[25] The phrase *de yi* is used in the fishnet allegory with this double meaning. The allegory is then not about how to get ideas, but about how to get rid of them.

The *Zhuangzi* discusses the problem of "ideas" or meanings quite frequently. The character *yi* is used more than fifty times in the book, and it is often used in semantic connection with words for "language" or "speech" (*yan*). Practically every time that the notion of *yi* ("meaning," "idea") appears in the sense of "the meaning of words" it has a *negative connotation* attached to it. Nowhere does the *Zhuangzi* say that it is good or desirable for the Daoist sage to have "ideas," but it often says the exact opposite: that the sage should *neither be stuck with words nor with ideas or meanings.* So why should the fishnet allegory and only the fishnet allegory—contradict the general Daoist tenor? A typical statement on words and meanings or ideas (*yi*) in the *Zhuangzi* goes as follows (with Guo Xiang's commentary in italics):

> What can be discussed with words is the coarseness of things. What can be reached with ideas is the refinement of things. That which cannot be discussed with words and that which cannot be investigated and reached with ideas neither belongs to the coarse nor to the refined.
>
> *Only nonpresence [wu]! What about the presence [you] of words and ideas? Well, words and ideas are present [you]. And that which words and ideas are about is nonpresence. So one looks for it in the realm of words and ideas, and then one enters the dominion of no-words and no-ideas and has finally arrived.*[26]

That which is neither coarse nor refined is the Dao. It is, as the *Zhuangzi* and Guo Xiang make perfectly clear, to be found neither in words, nor "meanings," nor "ideas" (*yi*). In order to arrive at the Dao, one has to go beyond *both* words and ideas. Accordingly, the Daoist master Tian Zi Fang describes the qualities of his teacher in the *Zhuangzi* as follows: "He made people's ideas disappear."[27] Ideas, as another passage in the *Zhuangzi* explains, are among the "six evils" that "confound the heart."[28] The Daoist sage, or the *zhen ren* ("true man"), attempts to discard all the intentions and ideas in his or her mind. The *Zhuangzi* says: "Even more than a sheep he/she casts off ideas."[29] The *Zhuangzi* is full of such declarations of the limitations of words *and* ideas or meanings. Why should the fishnet allegory then declare that the Daoist sage aims at "getting the meaning"?

Other early texts also show that Daoist philosophy was not simply about "getting ideas." The expression "No ideas!" (*wu yi*) appears as a philosophical motto. The *Liezi*[30] says: "No ideas!— Then the heart will be one."[31]

Given this philological and philosophical evidence, what does the fishnet allegory really say? How has it been understood by Daoist readers? One has to go back to the text itself and to Guo Xiang's commentary to answer this question. Guo Xiang comments on the fishnet allegory with only one sentence. He writes:

> When it comes to two sages having no ideas [*wu yi*], they will both have nothing to talk about.[32]

It is clear that for Guo Xiang the fishnet allegory does not say that the Daoist sage "gets the meaning" (*de yi*), but rather that he/she will be left with "no ideas"—this is just what he literally says. Guo Xiang obviously read the fishnet allegory in this way: Once a Daoist sage no longer has ideas, then he/she will also have attained the "desired" speechlessness. Thus, when two Daoist sages with empty minds meet, they can hardly start a philosophical conversation. There would simply be nothing to say! They could not discuss any "true meanings"! According to the "Aristotelian" interpretation of the fishnet allegory, the true philosopher will have to go beyond words in order to "get the meaning." According to Guo Xiang's Daoist reading of the fishnet allegory, the sage has to discard all ideas in order to realize Daoist silence.

With the help of Guo Xiang's commentary a Daoist reading of the fishnet allegory can be reconstructed. One can now understand the final sentence of the text in a somewhat less cryptic manner. In the light of Guo Xiang's interpretation the last sentence of the original can be simply read as: "How could I talk to somebody who has forgotten words?" Such a reading is philologically as plausible as Watson's, but is philosophically in accord with Guo Xiang's commentary. How and why would a Daoist sage, if he/she should meet another one, start arguing? Read in a Daoist way, the fishnet allegory is not about what sages "get," but rather about what they lose. This is perfectly in accord with the *Daodejing*, which repeatedly states not only that that the Dao and the sage are silent, but also that their strategy is one of gain by loss (see for instance *Daodejing*, chapter 48).

In the light of the basic Daoist teaching of "no words, no ideas," one can now reread the three parallel statements of the fishnet allegory. The first two of these are perfectly parallel images, both semantically and linguistically. The third sentence though, as is often the case with jokes or humoristic tales, contains a pun and breaks, in an ironic way, with the pattern the reader was made familiar with in the two preceding lines. The last line is, as pointed out above, ambiguous, and it is ambiguous because of the double meaning of the phrase *de yi*.

Let us read the fishnet allegory again from the beginning. Somewhat differently from Watson's translation, the first two sentences have as their main syntactic and semantic topics not fish and rabbits and the question of how to catch them, but rather fish traps and rabbit snares and the issue of how one can no longer be concerned with them. The text explicitly puts the snare and the trap in the first section, not the fish and the rabbit. So let us read the text in accord with its actual structure. The first sentences say in a more literal translation:

> [As to a] fish trap: [it is] the means to get hold of fish.
>> [One] gets the fish, and then [one can] forget the fish trap.
> [As to a] rabbit snare: [it is] the means to get hold of rabbits.
>> [One] gets the rabbit, and then [one can] forget the rabbit snare.

The text obviously focuses more on the traps and snares than on the fish and the rabbit. It tells us that they are instruments for getting something, and that they can only be of no more concern once they have helped us to get what they are made to get. So the text is first of all about instruments and the conditions under which we no longer care or depend on them. In order to be free from these instruments, one has to be in a state in which there is no need for them. When one has caught the fish or rabbit and, implicitly, when one is having them for a meal, one can put the snare and trap aside for a while. Only when you are no longer hungry will you not care about hunting. Let us look now at the third sentence of the fishnet allegory in a similarly literal translation:

> [As to] words: [they are] the means to get hold of ideas.
>   [One] gets the idea [*de yi*], and then [one can] forget the words.

This is the first possible reading of the line that contains the pun. In parallel to the first two sentences it says as much as: In order to be in a state of no longer caring about words, you must have understood their meaning. Only when you have "digested" the idea that the words "caught," will you no longer be "hungry" for the idea or concerned with the words. Once you've read the book and know the story, you can put it back on the shelf. This reading is somewhat similar to the standard interpretation—but it is quite incomplete, since it misses the crucial pun: *de yi* does not only mean "to get the idea" but, more commonly, "to get what one desires," or "to be satisfied." Thus the third line of the fishnet allegory also means:

> [As to] words: [they are] the means to get hold of ideas.
>   [One] gets one's desire [*de yi*], and then [one can] forget the words.

In this reading, the line says that the true condition for no longer caring about words is to get one's desire or to be satisfied. But what is the "desire" of the Daoist sage? What does it mean for him/her to be "satisfied"? As the *Zhuangzi* frequently states, the "desire" of the sage is to be without desires, namely to be without intentions, wishes, and ideas. *For the Daoist sage "to get one's desire"* (de yi) *means ironically, but exactly, to "have no desire"* (wu yi). The desire has to be *eaten up* in order to be fulfilled. It's fulfilled once it is gone! This is a basic Daoist philosophical paradox, and it is expressed in the pun of the fishnet allegory. To "get the idea" and "to get the meaning" (*de yi*) of Daoism is "to get one's desire" or "to be satisfied" (*de yi*)—but this means for the sage just "to have no ideas" (*wu yi*)! "Having" the idea has a double sense. It is like "having" a fish or a rabbit, or having a pizza and a beer—in English "having" a pizza and a beer actually means eating up the pizza and drinking up the beer. Once one has a pizza or a beer, one cannot have it any longer. The desire is fulfilled when it has disappeared. And the Daoist desire for ideas only disappears once the idea is "eaten up"—when it is no longer there. Getting the idea of the Dao means to get rid of any idea of it. As the *Daodejing* put it (chapter 78): *Right words are like the reverse.* Obviously, the "Aristotelian" reading of the fishnet allegory does not get this idea.

In a paradoxical yet Daoist manner the fishnet allegory can be read—in a free rendering that tries to convey the pun by using the word "to have" in the double sense of "possessing" and "eating up"—as follows:

> A fish trap is the means to get hold of fish.
>> You can only forget about the fish trap once you've had your fish.
> A rabbit snare is the means to get hold of rabbits.
>> You can only forget about the rabbit snare once you've had your rabbit.
> Words are the means to get hold of ideas.
>> You can only forget about the words once you've had your ideas.
> How could I talk to somebody who has forgotten words?
> *When it comes to two sages having no ideas, they will both have nothing to talk about.*

The fishnet allegory is by no means about how to catch and keep some deep thoughts or ideas. It is, on the contrary, about the method of getting rid of thoughts and ideas in order to arrive at a perfect Daoist silence. It is about how to become permanently satisfied and to completely eliminate the hunger for the next dish of meanings and language.

The famous Chinese poet Yang Wanli (1127–1206) has, more than a millennium after the origin of the *Zhuangzi*, applied the paradoxical Daoist idea of "No ideas!" to an equally paradoxical theory of poetry. He gives, quite in parallel to the fishnet allegory, some instructions on how to write poetry without thinking:

How is poetry made?—One may cherish the words, this should be the essential!—Or rather, the good poet may get rid of words and cherish ideas!—Or rather, the good poet may get rid of ideas!—But when both words and ideas are gotten rid of, where's poetry then?—Well, poetry is just there where words and ideas are gotten rid of.—But if it's like that, what does poetry consist of?

Concerning a good meal, doesn't the tea come after the sweet dishes? Who wouldn't long for the sweet dishes—but these taste good at first, and then finally they taste bad. And when it comes to the tea, it tastes bitter to people, but this bitterness does not linger on and begins to taste good. That's how it is with poetry.[33]

Good poetry, the poet says, is without meaning and, so to speak, without sense. It might seem "insipid" at first, but unlike the "sweet" poetry full of words and ideas, the "insipid" poetry does not spoil one's stomach and tastes. Like a good tea will neutralize all the different tastes of a good meal, good poetry will neutralize the thousands of words and thoughts one comes upon in life. Good tea does not stir up all the tastes of the meal one has just had, and good poetry does not stir up all the words, feelings, and thoughts that one deals with on a daily basis. Good tea and good poetry are similar in their soothing and emptying effects. Daoist philosophy is meant to work likewise: it will not lead one to great words and exciting ideas, it will rather finish these off.

The Happy Fish—Or: Joy without Joy

A short but rather well-known story in the *Zhuangzi* contains a discussion about the happiness of fish. While Zhuangzi and his philosopher friend and opponent Huizi are out on a leisurely stroll, a dispute arises between them:

Zhuangzi and Huizi were rambling around [*you*] at the bridge across the Hao river. Zhuangzi said: "Out come the minnows and drift along [*you*], so free and easy. That's the happiness of fish!" Huizi said: "You are not a fish. Whence do you know about the happiness of fish?" Zhuangzi replied: "You are not me. Whence do you know that I don't know about the happiness of fish?" Huizi answered: "I am not you, so I surely don't know about you. You are surely not a fish, and this proves completely that you don't know about the happiness of fish." Zhuangzi said: "Let's go back to where we started. When you said 'Whence do you know about the happiness of fish' you asked me the question already knowing that I knew. I knew it from up above the Hao."[34]

Just like many other allegories in the *Zhuangzi*, this story includes several puns (which unfortunately do not receive appropriate recognition in many English translations). The crucial pun occurs in the first line of the story, and understanding it is necessary for understanding the debate that unfolds in the following sentences. Zhuangzi's and Huizi's stroll is described as "rambling around," which is *you* in Chinese (not the same character as *you* meaning "presence"!). This word is also used in the title of the first chapter of the *Zhuangzi*: "Going Rambling without a Destination" (*xiao yao you*) and is an important term for the "lifestyle" of the Daoist sage. When Zhuangzi starts talking about the fish in the river Hao, he uses the very same word for their "drifting along." Both the men's wandering and the swimming of the fish is thus described with a Daoist *terminus technicus* for the complete absorption in one's natural environment or in one's natural place and position. If one "rambles" free and easy, one has no friction whatsoever with one's surroundings and so is part of a seamless, easygoing process. The notion of *you* expresses how it feels to be part of a perfect scenario—it is the perfect Daoist "feeling," so to speak.

The second pun is based upon the ambiguity of Huizi's question, which initiates the philosophical dispute: "Whence do you know about the happiness of fish?" This can be—as it was obviously intended by Huizi—a rhetorical question meaning simply, "How should it ever be possible for you to know about the happiness of fish?" Huizi seems not to be merely asking Zhuangzi *how* he can have such knowledge, but denying *that* he can have it at all. Huizi is addressing an epistemological issue: One should not claim to have knowledge to which one has no access.

Zhuangzi, at first, takes Huizi's philosophical attack seriously and tries to defeat Huizi by his own means—but this attempt is not successful. His argument that Huizi cannot claim any knowledge about him—not even his claim about the fish—is defeated by Huizi's reprisal that this argument—the invalidity of knowledge claims about realms one is somehow separate from—proves Huizi, and not Zhuangzi, to be correct. It is epistemologically problematic to claim such knowledge, and thus Zhuangzi's claim to know the happiness of the fish may be some "poetic" expression of one's feelings strolling along the river, but it cannot be taken seriously as a philosophical statement.

Zhuangzi, having lost the epistemological dispute, twists the whole philosophical direction of the discussion in the last sentence of the dialogue. He plays with the ambiguity of Huizi's initial question. Both in English and Chinese the question "*Whence* do you know about (*an zhi*) the happiness of fish?" can also mean "From where do you know about the happiness of fish?" It can be a question like "From where did you see that fish hiding behind the stone?" If the question is understood in this way, it is not a rhetorical question, but a real one. Literally, Huizi had indeed asked this question, and by asking this question—although not intentionally but linguistically—acknowledged that Zhuangzi knew about the happiness of fish whereas he himself did not. Thus Zhuangzi now answers Huizi's question in a literal way: "From where did you see the happiness of the fish?—"Oh, I just see it from here, from my perspective while strolling along and above the Hao river." And this has again a double meaning: It means, first of all, "I simply see the fish from here where I am" but it also means: "I see that the fish are happy, because while I am rambling here (*you*) and they are drifting there (*you*), we are actually sharing the same 'lifestyle.' We are both *you*ing! That's how I know what they feel."

This pun with the term *you* explains whence Zhuangzi knows about the happiness of fish. With his final sentence he answers Huizi in a Daoist way. He fails to convincingly prove his knowledge claim using Huizi's epistemology, but with the final sentence he alludes to the notion of *you*—and thus supports his claim in a particular Daoist manner. Guo Xiang's commentary to the fishnet allegory explains this Daoist "epistemology":

> Well, what things are born into and what they rejoice in—heaven and earth cannot change this position, and Yin and Yang cannot take back this livelihood. Therefore it cannot be called strange if one can know what beings born into the water are happy with from [being familiar with] what beings born on land rejoice in.[35]

With Guo Xiang's help, Zhuangzi's point is elucidated: Zhuangzi is a human being and his way to *you* is to ramble around carefree on the land. Fish have a different position and "livelihood," they have a different place in the scenario of Dao, they have a different nature, and accordingly, they have a different way to *you*—they *you* by drifting along in water. Each being has its own natural place in its environment, and Zhuangzi can only feel like fish in the water while on land. Both species have their respective "elements." When Zhuangzi claimed to know about the happiness of fish, he did not claim to be able to feel the exact same feeling. He was just saying: I feel perfect by rambling around, and the fish feel perfect by drifting around. Both are *you*—but two kinds of *you*, a fish-*you*, and a human-*you*. There are different kinds of "happiness," a fish-happiness, and a man-happiness, and these are not exchangeable! The fish will never be able to ramble on the land and feel perfectly happy there, and it would be a miracle for a man to drift around in the water just as happily as fish.[36] Both kinds of happiness are entirely *different and separate*, but they are both *equally* in perfect accord with the Dao.

Comparing this story with the butterfly dream allegory one might say: Just as the butterfly can be perfectly content and in its element during the time of the dream, and as Zhuang Zhou can be perfectly content and in his element while being awake, so also the fish in the water and the human being on land can be perfectly content and in their elements. They do not know exactly how the other feels, but they can know that each of them can rejoice in what they are. Because one can be self-content in a dream, one can know that one can be self-content when awake; and because a man can be self-content on land, one can know that fish can be self-content in water.

The happiness of the fish is the happiness of complete absorption in one's natural environment or in one's natural place and position. This happiness is attainable for fish, humans, and butterflies. But this happiness is not just some kind of emotional "joy." The perfect happiness of the fish or man is that they lose themselves in their respective element. And if they lose themselves, they will also be able to lose their joy. The perfect Daoist happiness is joy without joy. It is not tied to any particular emotional sensation and is not felt in a specific way. The *Zhuangzi* also says: "Utmost happiness is without happiness."[37] A Daoist sage does not only forget words, ideas, and him/herself, he/she also forgets any particular kind of happiness. The perfect emotional quality is a feeling one no longer feels. A Daoist sage takes on the "zero-perspective" of joy—he/she will know about the happiness of men and fish while enjoying the "utmost happiness without happiness" him/herself.

Issues

Daoist images and allegories were meant as materials for the exercises of Daoist practice. They had a didactic function. With the help of these images and allegories one was supposed to learn how to follow the patterns of the Dao and how to transform oneself into a Daoist sage. Using the image of the wheel, it can be said that these materials were meant to teach one how to get into the position of the hub and how to keep the wheel running.

Daoist teachings were supposed to be for various practical tasks. The main "disciplines" of early Daoist practice were the organization of the state and of the body. They were a kind of architectural concept for the construction of the perfect scenario. The philosophy, accordingly, provided descriptions of what Daoist "education" in the fields of political and bodily cultivation (as well as in other areas) could achieve. It provided blueprints of how to solve a variety of issues in a Daoist way.

1. The State

In the *Zhuangzi*, political issues are, for the most part, regarded as something quite unimportant. In fact, many passages in the *Zhuangzi* ridicule political activity and the strife for political position. One example of this general attitude is the following story about Zhuangzi and Huizi—Zhuangzi's philosopher friend with whom he debated about the happiness of fish:

> When Huizi was chief minister of the state of Liang, Zhuangzi went to visit him. Someone told Huizi: "Zhuangzi is coming, he wants

your place as chief minister." At this Huizi was frightened, and
searched throughout the state for three days and nights. Zhuangzi
then went to visit him. "In the south there is a bird," he said, "its
name is the phoenix, do you know of it? The phoenix came up from
the South Sea to fly to the North Sea; it would rest on no trees but
the rare *sterculia*, would not eat nothing but the finest seed of bamboo, would drink only from the sweetest springs. Once an owl had
just found a rotten mouse, and as the phoenix flew over, it looked up
and glared at it, saying 'Shoo!' Now am I to take it that for the sake
of that Liang country of yours you want to shoo at me?"[1]

Zhuangzi did not care about politics. Politics and political positions were as attractive to him as a rotten mouse to a phoenix. This
is quite different from the *Daodejing*, which was in fact once
meant as a guidebook for political leaders. Many chapters in the
Daodejing explicitly address rulers and kings; the early manuscripts
were found in the tombs of ancient Chinese regents; and the "I"
that appears in the text is to be understood as the "I" of the ideal
ruler with whom the potential reader—namely the prospective
leader—was supposed to identify.

It was in such a strict political sense that the *Daodejing* was
understood by Hanfeizi (280–233 BCE). Hanfeizi wrote a book
bearing his name that unfolds a political teaching of ruling by punishment and reward. The ruler is always hidden in the background
of the political process itself and leads the state without actual
political interference. His main duty is to supervise and judge the
political activities of others. This so-called "Legalist" philosophy of
government was developed by Hanfeizi in direct connection with
the political teachings of the *Daodejing*. Two entire chapters of
this book are exclusively dedicated to quoting and commenting on
verses of this Daoist classic.

The strategy of ruling that is of crucial importance in the
Hanfeizi—and that also plays a role in Confucian political
thought—can be summarized with the famous motto found in the
Daodejing: "doing nothing and nothing is undone" (*wu wei er wu
bu wei*, chapter 37, 48). In the political realm this was supposed to
mean that if the ruler would not take on any tasks himself, all tasks
would then be more or less automatically taken on by his subjects.
Whereas the Daoists believed in the natural efficacy of this strategy
of passivity on behalf of the ruler, the Legalists combined it with
the institution of *penal law* (*fa* in Chinese)—which gained them

their name. According to Legalist doctrine, the ideal ruler rules by impartially letting the penal law preside and judge over his subjects' actions. If their actions and performances were good and correct, the law would reward them, if not, the law would punish them. The ruler was a sort of manifestation of the penal law. Since he himself did not act, he was the only one who could not be judged by the law. He then was, in a certain sense, the single executive of the law—and also its executioner.

Both Legalism and Huang-Lao-Daoism conceived of the law as exercising the power of the Dao. The *Four Classics of the Yellow Emperor* begins with the sentence: "The Dao gives birth to the law" (*dao sheng fa*). In other branches of Daoist philosophy, however, the conception of penal law as the executive power of the Dao plays only a very minor role, if any at all. Most Daoist political philosophers believed that the Dao would by itself be able to give rise to a natural and spontaneous political order. If only the regent would not interfere, the perfect political scenario would be established just "self-so" (*ziran*).

The passive role of the regent—his motionlessness—corresponds to the activity and motion of his subjects. While the ruler has only the duty of being the center of power, the subjects have to perform the myriad tasks. In the realm of action it is important that all tasks harmoniously complement each other so that a complete political organism will emerge. For the perfect political process to take place, a strict distinction between tasks is necessary—to express it in the terminology of the butterfly dream allegory. While the ruler stays passively at the center of all action, all actions are coordinated by being clearly distinct from one another. The order of the political process depends on the subjects doing what is theirs to do—and only what is theirs to do—at the right place and time. There is a passage in the *Zhuangzi* that describes, in even more detail than the *Daodejing*, how the passivity of the ruler and the activity of the subjects combine into a most efficient political organism:

> Thus the people of old esteemed nonaction. Would, however, those on top not act and also those below also not act, then those on top and those below would exercise the same "Power" [*de*]. And if those on top and those below exercise the same Power, then there are no subjects. But if those on top would act and those below would also act, then those on top and those below would share the same "Way"

[*dao*]. And if those on top and those below share the same Way, then there is no ruler. Those on top have to not-act to make use of the world. Those below have to act to be made of use for the world. This is the unchanging "Way" [*dao*].[2]

This Daoist concept of the complementarity of action and non-action was modified by Hanfeizi in a Legalist way. The following story from his work illustrates quite drastically how the nonacting ruler has to continuously supervise the correct distribution of action among his subjects:

> Once in the past marquis Zhao of Han got drunk and fell asleep. The keeper of the royal hat, seeing that the marquis was cold, laid a robe over him. When the marquis awoke, he was pleased and asked his attendants, "Who covered me with a robe?" "The keeper of the hat," they replied. The marquis thereupon punished both the keeper of the royal hat and the keeper of the royal robe. He punished the keeper of the robe for failing to do his duty, and the keeper of the hat for over-stepping his office. It was not that he did not dislike the cold, but he considered the trespass of one official upon the duties of another to be a greater danger than cold.[3]

The keeper of the hat was punished—and this could well have meant by death—because he transgressed the limits of his duties. The keeper of the robe was punished equally because he did not fulfill his duties. It is important to note that according to Legalist and Huang-Lao-Daoist political thought the action of the marquis cannot be understood as being despotic or cruel—it is rather an expression of his harmony with the Dao. The order of the world is dependant on the strict distinctions between the activities in the world. The ruler has to take care, especially at his court at the center of the world, that these distinctions are not transgressed and that everyone lives up to his or her task. If these distinctions are not respected, and if the tasks are not fulfilled, then the order of the world will break down—the Dao will no longer prevail.

The single one who does not act—the ruler—does not only have to be void of activity, he also has to be empty of emotion. He is supposed to have feelings neither of revenge nor of mercy—both kinds of feelings would indicate partiality. The ruler is not supposed to be influenced by the kindness of the keeper of the hat who covered him with a robe. He has to eliminate all personal feelings and attachments. He has to empty his heart in order to be a true manifestation of the impersonal and impartial Dao. From a Legalist point of view, the ruler acts in accord with the Dao when he executes even those who violate the "natural" distinctions of action by doing him a personal favor.

Even though it may seem odd or shocking to the present-day reader, this "bloody" Legalist story is built around a core Daoist philosophical motif that can also be found in the *Zhuangzi*'s "peaceful" butterfly dream allegory: order by perfect distinction. Guo Xiang, commenting on the butterfly dream story, says that the reason why the process of change can be perfectly harmonious is that "distinctions are firmly established and not that there are no distinctions." Likewise, the Legalist and Huang-Lao-Daoist ruler has to make sure that order prevails in the political realm by keeping distinctions intact. The Daoist ruler tries to establish and maintain distinctions of social activity by pure nonaction, while the Legalist ruler tries to reach the same goal by a strict penal code that is supposed to be the direct manifestation of the Dao.

In the words of the *Daodejing* (chapter 57), the ideal ruler should practice the following principles of government:

> I do not act,
>> and the people change by themselves.
> I love stillness,
>> and the people correct themselves.
> I am without task,
>> and the people prosper by themselves.
> I desire without desire,
>> and the people turn to simplicity by themselves.

If the sage ruler "loves stillness," the people will "by themselves" follow the right way. The ruler has to ensure that there will be enough for everybody in the state to live on, but the prospering of the people will make them turn to the "simplicity" (*pu*) of the "uncarved wood." People fulfill their tasks, and they will have no desire to leave their places. The self-restriction of the ruler makes the people modest and content. The ideal Daoist state is depicted in the famous eightieth chapter of the *Daodejing*:

A small state, few people.

Let there be a militia and weapons,
    but people do not use them.
People take death seriously
    and migrating is far from their mind.
There are boats and carriages
    which no one rides.
There are shields and swords
    which no one takes up.
Let people return to the use of knotted cords for writing.

Sweet be the food.
Beautiful be the clothing.
Happy be the customs.
Peaceful be the homes.

Neighboring states are within distance of sight,
    and the sounds of chicken and dogs are mutually heard.
But people reach old age and die
    without traveling back and forth.

The ideal Daoist state has everything that is necessary for a life—but nothing used to cross the border. Prosperity does not overstep the limits of a simple lifestyle. No harmful desires will arise. Everybody in the ideal Daoist state is content within its realm. No one intends even to go to the villages of the neighboring state that are only a short distance away. If desires should arise, the ruler will "subdue them with the nameless, uncarved wood" of simplicity, as chapter 37 of the *Daodejing* says. And chapter 32 adds: "Without issuing orders, the people will by themselves enter into an equilibrium."

The ideal Daoist ruler rules in accordance with the Dao. He is the hub of the social wheel, single, motionless, central, and empty of qualities or personal characteristics. He has no personal belongings and no one has a special relation with him. He is hidden and no one knows him personally: "Of the best of all rulers people will only know that he exists" (*Daodejing*, chapter 17). The ideal ruler does not step beyond his door or look out of his windows (chapter 47); he does not talk (chapters 14, 23), and does not act: "I am quiet and I do not show any sign" (chapter 20). The Daoist ruler has "the heart of an idiot" (chapter 20) because there is nothing in it, no specific thought, desire, or inclination. "The ordinary people are bright and clear, I alone am dark and obscure. The ordinary people are distinct. I alone am undifferentiated" (chapter 20). It is by being nameless, invisibly hidden, and unmoved that the ruler unites the state.

The Daoist ruler claims his position with paradoxical language. The designations he uses are negative. He is the abandoned and the orphaned, the idiot and the obscure. These self-depreciations signal his entitlement to be the head of the state. The forty-third chapter of the *Daodejing* ends with the words: "To take on the unfavorable in the state, this is to be king of the world. Right words are like the reverse." Those who declare themselves to be in the lowest place, in the context of Daoist imagery, are fit for the highest position. The paradoxical reversal is a rule for Daoist political rhetoric: Loss is gain, and to renounce means to claim. The conception of gain by loss relates back to even older Chinese religious and political rites. The Chinese term *rang*, which is often used in ritualistic and Confucian texts, is a predecessor of the Daoist concept of change and reversal and of its paradoxical strategies. The great French Sinologist Marcel Granet observed: "The rites employed to expel the old year and install the new bear the name of *rang*. *Rang* signifies to banish: the same word also means to renounce, but to renounce in order to have. The Chinese sovereign scarcely exists, who, at the moment of assuming his authority, did not act as though he desired to renounce it."[4] For the ruler, the Daoist rule of reversal means that he establishes and holds on to his power by not displaying it at all. If he would display it, he would endanger himself and the order of the state. The one who is best in the Daoist art of holding back will succeed in becoming ruler. Chapter 66 of the *Daodejing* declares:

> If the sage wishes to be above the people,
>   he must put himself below them in his words.
> If he wishes to be at the front of the people,
>   He must put himself behind them as a person.

Not only the functioning of the wheel but also that of the state is subject to the Daoist motto expressed in chapter 40 of the *Daodejing*: "Reversal is the movement of the Dao."

2. The Body (Of Infants and Corpses)

In ancient China, the state and the physical body were commonly
believed to be analogously structured. Huang-Lao-Daoism high-
lighted this analogy within the specter of Daoist philosophy. The
text of the *Guanzi* contains many materials believed to be connected to Huang-Lao thought. The two chapters within this book
concerning the "The Art of the Heart" (*Xinshu shang* and *Xinshu
xia*), as well as the chapters about "Purifying the Heart" (*Baixin*)
and "Inner Workings" (*Neiye*), explain in detail some of the parallels between the body and the state. Similar to Hanfeizi's transformation of the philosophical content of the *Daodejing* into a
concrete teaching of government, the above mentioned chapters
of the *Guanzi*, and other writings attributable to Huang-Lao
thought, transformed elements of the *Daodejing* into a teaching of
physical and social cultivation. The first of the two chapters on
"The Art of the Heart" says:

> In the body, the heart holds the position of the ruler. The functions
> of the nine apertures correspond to the separate responsibilities of
> officials. The ears and eyes are the organs for seeing and hearing. If
> the heart does not interfere with the activities of seeing and hearing,
> the organs will be able to maintain their separate functions. Now if the
> heart is full of desires, the eyes will not see when things pass by nor
> will the ears hear when there are sounds. Therefore it is said: "If the
> person on high departs from the Way (*dao*), those below will be lax
> in their work." Therefore it is said: "The art of the heart lies in con-
> trolling the apertures by non-action." [5]

The above passage shows how a Daoist structure for the perfect
scenario of order—an empty and passive center dominating an
active and distinctly divided periphery—could be simultaneously
applied to the body and the state. The same vocabulary (the same
Chinese words are used respectively for "organ" and "official"
[*guan*] and for "organic function" and "professional function"
[*zhi*]) is used for both fields of order. The "art of the heart" is a
copy of the "art of government."

Confucian and even pre-Confucian conceptions of the art of
government had been closely tied to conceptions of the personal
cultivation of the ruler. It was believed that a state would only be
successful if the ruler was good at purifying himself morally and

bodily. The ancient Chinese idea that a ruler has to bring his body in order before he can order the state also appears in the *Daodejing*. Chapter 54, in particular, describes (in a style quite reminiscent of the Confucian *Great Learning*) how the cultivation of the ruler's body will result in the cultivation first of the social body and then of the whole world.

In the course of the Han Dynasty, and especially during its later half, there emerged many conceptions, theories, legends, cults, and even political movements that were related to earlier Daoist ideas on how to cultivate the body. These were the melting pot for the rich practices of Daoism that evolved through the centuries and are still alive today. Recently, Daoist practices of bodily cultivation are sometimes subsumed under the somewhat misleading category of "spirituality." This is misleading, because at least early Daoism focused more on physical aspects than on "spiritual" ones, or rather, the "spiritual" was conceived of as a kind of extension of or complement to bodily functions. It is not without reason that the eminent scholar Kristofer Schipper has named his concise survey of Daoism (or of Daoist practice) *Les corps taoiste—The Daoist Body*.[6] One might well say that, generally speaking, Daoist practice did not so much strive for "spiritual" transformation as it did for bodily transformation. A primary goal of Daoist practice, especially in pre-Buddhist times, was to attain longevity and possibly even cultivate the body in such a way that one would become an immortal (*xian*).

One of the most important ancient Chinese "physical" notions is the concept of *Qi*. This concept was—and still is—crucial for both Daoist theories of the body and bodily practices. The word Qi has been translated into English as "vital force," "activating force," "matter," "energy," and in various combinations of these terms. Other translators have suggested Greek terms like *pneuma*. A more colloquial translation is "breath." The word is still part of everyday language in China and is an element of many very common words such as *tian-qi* or "weather," which literally means "heaven's Qi." Qi is a "something" that streams through and blows through the whole world. Everything is made "alive" by Qi—not only humans, animals, and plants, but also such things as paintings and stones. It is believed to be the kind of "vital force" that is "breathing" in everything that exists. Accordingly, in China cultivation of the body meant—not only in Daoism but in general—cultivation of the body's Qi. Many techniques were developed to "order" the flow of Qi within the body, to manage it, to somehow guide or canalize it. A generic term for these techniques is Qi Gong—the Qi exercise—which is becoming increasingly popular in the West. These exercises are supposed to enhance the efficacy of the Qi streaming through the body and to produce a variety of healthy effects. They also help the body to perform certain "tricks" that could not be done without training. Qi Gong can consist of breathing exercises, but it can also entail, for instance, dietary or sexual practices. An important aspect of "working with" Qi is to let it flow "naturally." The flow of Qi as the flow of "vital energy" is supposed to be as unimpeded as possible. If Qi could flow without friction, then the body would lose no energy and might become a constant and permanent functioning.

Exercises of the Qi are already an issue in the *Daodejing*. Three chapters mention this term. Chapter 10 describes—quite poetically, but also rather vaguely—how the Daoist sage cultivates the body and the state. In this context it is suggested that one "con*centr*ate (*zhuan*) the Qi"—which may well be taken literally in the sense of making it continuously *circulate around a center*. Chapter 55 of the *Daodejing* admonishes the heart, that is, the bodily regent, not to "force" the Qi. Like in the state, Daoist control or guidance is not one of active interference, but rather an inactive "letting it go." It is only in this way that the Qi energy will constitute a scenario of bodily "harmony," as chapter 42 indicates.

While the concept of circulating Qi energy is essential for Chinese and Daoist concepts of the functioning of the body, it is, as stated above, by no means limited to bodily concerns. Qi circulates everywhere. Qi flows through the body as it flows through a landscape or a painting. One always has to be aware of the invisible flow of Qi, not only when cultivating one's body, but also when finding a place for a home or—even more importantly—a tomb. This is the art of *Feng Shui*. Artists also have to take into account the flow of Qi when they create a scene on paper or silk. The analogy between the body and a natural or "artificial" landscape leads to an understanding of the body as a kind of world in itself. The body is not just an individual thing living with the world as its outside environment—the body itself is a whole "landscape." In this way, the body is not only like a state, which has to be

ordered through the division of functions and "bureaucratic" hierarchies, but also it is like a living landscape whose flow of energy
should be made aesthetic and harmonious.

Daoists tried in many ways to transform the body into a field
of permanent energy-flow. Whereas the "classical" philosophical
texts hardly include any concrete recipes for such a transformation, a wide range of detailed instructions for bodily cultivation is
introduced in the books and scriptures of Daoist practice. Still,
mainly philosophical works, like the *Daodejing* and the *Zhuangzi*,
do contain some essential elements or models of Daoist bodily
theories and practices. These were the main source for later developments of Daoism, and so both trends share many concepts and
images. However, these images can have different meanings in
different contexts. While practical Daoism was always focused on
the physical body, philosophical Daoism tended to look at the
body in a more symbolic way. For philosophical Daoism the idea
of immortality is less connected to the concrete human body than
it is in practical Daoism. Daoist practitioners often believed that
they could actually transform their own body into an imperishable
organism. In philosophical Daoism, the long-living sage is a more
metaphorical figure. It was hardly the aim of those like Zhuangzi
to end up as an Immortal who lived far away in the mountains.

The images of the Immortal in the *Daodejing*, as well as in the
Zhuangzi, seem somewhat contradictory at first sight. Those sages
who have attained bodily perfection tend to be portrayed at one
time as *infants* and at another time as *old men*. The common structure shared by these seemingly contradictory images may be a clue
for an understanding of the concept of the body in philosophical
Daoism.

Chapter 10 of the *Daodejing* immediately connects the image
of the infant with the "concentration" of Qi:

> When you concentrate the Qi and attain softness,
>   can you be like an infant?

The concentration of Qi gives the body the "softness" and suppleness of a baby. These are also the characteristics of another
Daoist image discussed above—water. The body of the infant is
not only soft and supple, it is at the same time also potentially
tough and untiring, as chapter 55 of the *Daodejing* explains:

One who embodies the fullness of Power [*de*]
>   is like an infant.
Wasps, scorpions, vipers, and snakes
>   do not bite it.
Birds of prey and wild beasts
>   do not seize it.
Bones and muscles are soft and weak,
>   but its grip is firm.
It does not know yet about the joining of the male and the female,
>   but its penis is erect.
This is the maximum of vital essence.
It screams all day
>   without getting hoarse.
This is the maximum of harmony.

The infant practices nonaction. It does not arouse the aggressive instincts of dangerous wild animals. It also incorporates the utmost bodily potency—including sexual potency—without letting these potencies out of its body. (In a sexual context, this is similar to the Daoist practice of holding back ejaculation in order to increase one's inner energy levels.) This unspent "fullness of power" enables the infant to have a tight grasp and to scream without harming its voice. The image of the infant is practically also an image of the embryo—an image of the human being that has not begun to live in any friction with its environment. It is the image of a human being in which all powers are potential and no power has yet been exerted or lost. There is not the slightest "wear and tear" that comes with the accumulation of years. The embryo is without openings (see *Daodejing*, chapters 52 and 56), and thus it is as perfectly closed in itself as Hundun, the legendary "Emperor of the Center."[7] The human being, like Hundun, starts to die once it has bodily openings. The bodily openings together with the four limbs are called the "thirteen companions of life." They enable human beings to move, they are the vehicles for metabolism and procreation—but they also make human beings mortal.[8] They let energy "leak out." The human body as a living body is naturally, at the same time, a dying body. Chapter 50 of the *Daodejing* puts it in this way:

>   Going out into life.
>   Going in into death.

> The companions of life are thirteen.
> The companions of death are thirteen.
> For the human beings moving on living their lives
>   they all become thirteen spots of approaching death.

Movement and a life of activity are equivalent to the exhaustion of one's vital energies. Accordingly, a minimum of movement and activity results in minimizing one's mortality. The permanent body therefore resembles the least mobile and active of all human beings; it resembles the rather amorphous embryo or infant. Here, potency is still pure potency for it has not yet taken on a specific form or shape. The infant, or, more specifically the embryo, has the characteristics of a Daoist immortal. To become an immortal is to return to this state. Here, there is life potential and no "spots of death." A being that has no spots of death cannot be killed—not even by beasts and wild animals. Chapter 50 of the *Daodejing* goes on to say regarding these experts of life: "the rhinoceros has no spot to jab its horn / the tiger has no spot to put its claws."

One can find another "body type" of the Daoist sage. This is repeatedly described in the *Zhuangzi* as "a body like dry wood and a heart like dead ashes."[9] As opposed to the softness and suppleness of the infant, this image presents the Daoist sage as brittle and burnt out. All potency is gone. No more movement can be expected. The sage now appears as a very old man—or as a corpse.

The image of the infant or embryo and the image of the old man or corpse share a common feature: They both represent a state at the fringes of life —and at the fringes of death. They represent a state in between life and death. The infant or the embryo does *not yet* really live (the "infant that does not yet smile" in chapter 20 of the *Daodejing*) whereas the old man or the corpse *no longer* really lives. The unborn does not yet have any "spots of death"—no "openings" to the outside world- -and the corpse *no longer* has any "spots of death"—in ancient China the facial openings of the dead were ritually closed by covering them with jade. Both the image of the unborn and of the corpse are images of the body as a closed organism without any "wear or tear." They are not understood as opposites but as the two poles of life, the turning points between life and death. They both represent the center of the circle of life and death, and thus they both represent permanence. In the *Zhuangzi*, both images are combined in a single passage of text. This passage is spoken by Laozi, whose name literally means *Old Child* and who is supposed to have been born with the features of an old man. In the *Zhuangzi*, he gives the following answer to a question about the "preservation of life":

> Can you be a child? A child moves without knowing what is being done [by it]. It goes, but it does not know where. Your body should be like the branch of a dried up tree, your heart should be like dead ashes.[10]

The infant and the old man are images of the preservation of life because they do not lose any vital forces. They are closed bodies that do not leak energy. This is why they both represent the ideal of Daoist bodily cultivation. The Daoist transformation of the body aims at reaching the closure of an embryo or a corpse.

This closure transforms the body into a kind of landscape, into a region that is a complete world to itself. To transform the body into such a complete and closed landscape means that there is no "beyond," no outside or environment. A relation between the body and the environment always brings friction. Bodily closure means to transform the body into a self-sustaining "microcosm." In this case the body is transformed from being a vanishing element within a process of change into this process as such. Therefore the Daoist transformation of the body into a "world" or a landscape also means the transformation of the body from an individual element into a nonindividual and complex whole.

Bodily transformation into a complex whole results in the extinction of individual features and of individuality as such. In the *Zhuangzi*, the transformation into "dry wood and dead ashes" is therefore also equated with the loss of the ego.[11] Being an ego implies being an ego next to other egos who are not one's own ego. To live as an ego among egos means to live in the world of multiplicity, not in the world of singularity. In regard to the image of the wheel, one can say that being an I among many means to be in the realm of the spokes as opposed to the hub and thus the whole wheel. The individual I has to be transformed into a singular whole. It has to be transformed into a singularity without openings, which includes all multiplicity and change within it—as opposed to being an individual part beside many others that are mere elements of change. One has to transform one's body into a whole wheel, so to speak, into a whole scenario that includes all potentials within it. The body will then be without a specific form or shape, but will include the potential of all shapes and forms. It will keep all potencies within it and allow none to escape.

Chinese art has portrayed these Daoist immortals who transformed themselves into an infant, into an old man, into a scenery, and into a microcosm. In his book *The Daoist Body*, Kristofer Schipper discusses a representation of an immortal by the famous Chinese painter Liang Kai (twelfth century CE). The painting is believed to be intended as a portrait of Laozi himself. In this painting, Laozi looks more like a mountain than a man. He looks like a mountain in the mist, and he is painted, as Schipper explains, with the techniques of landscape painting, not of portrait painting. Schipper also remarks that Laozi's expressionless face is reminiscent of a newborn baby.[12] All of these observations are certainly correct. One might only add that Laozi not only looks like a baby and a mountain, but also like an old man! Liang Kai's Laozi is *without age*. He is an infant and an old man, an embryo and a corpse—and this is why he is also a whole mountain scene, young and old at the same time, a complete scenario of the Dao.

FIGURE 3
An Immortal. Painted by Liang Kai (twelfth century CE).
Palace Museum, Taibei.

3. Life and Death

Many Daoists strived for bodily immortality. They believed that
people such as the one depicted in Liang Kai's painting actually
existed. Philosophical Daoism, however, tended to view the bodily
transformation of an I into a body-cosmos as an image of how to
deal with life and death. Unlike Daoist practice, philosophical
Daoism was not so much concerned with physical longevity as with
proposing a conception of life and death that would rid one of the
fear of mortality. Thus, Daoist practice and Daoist philosophy held
seemingly contradictory attitudes towards the human body and
death. These differences have been noted by many Sinologists. The
German Sinologist Wolfgang Bauer, for instance, distinguished
between "a heroic indifference towards dying" propagated in
philosophical texts and an utmost esteem of physical life as
expressed in the ideals of longevity and immortality.[13]

In spite of these internal differences, Daoist thought in both its
dimensions can be understood—just like many other philosophies
and religions—as a reaction to the inevitability of death, as an
attempt at compensating for human mortality. Daoism offers its
adherents a belief, an attitude, or a practice that is able to alleviate
the terror of the prospect and presence of death. While practical
Daoism offers bodily immortality, philosophical Daoism offers a
concept to take away that which makes the idea of death so
uncomfortable. Both ways of coping with death have a decisive
characteristic in common: they both operate with an ideal of permanence—only on different levels. The philosophical indifference
towards death and the practical quest for the everlasting body can
be interpreted as two variations—a macrocosmic and a microcosmic one—of the same Daoist conception of uninterrupted duration that leaves no room for an absolute death. Daoist practitioners
tried to transform their bodies into a permanent microcosmic
"landscape," while philosophical Daoists constructed a permanent
cycle of life and death in which the Daoist was supposed to find a
most favorable position.

Among Daoist texts, the *Zhuangzi* is probably the one that
most intensely focuses on the issue of death—particularly if it is
read along with the commentary by Guo Xiang. In the following,
I will attempt to describe the Daoist philosophy of life and death
as it appears in the *Zhuangzi*.

The distinction between life and death corresponds to other distinctions: it is introduced in connection with the distinctions between bright and dark, sun and moon, beginning and end, going out and going in, full and empty, heaven and earth, and is also used in analogy with the distinctions between the four seasons and, particularly, with the distinction between being awake and dreaming. These distinctions are always conceived of as complementary units. Brightness and darkness, day and night, and the four seasons combine into a complementary whole by changing into each other. Likewise, life and death are consecutive phases that constitute a temporal circle. A crucial idea of the Daoist conception of life and death is that no phase is privileged. All phases are equally valid and real. They replace each other because they are parts of the natural process of change. There is no hierarchy, for it is not the case that one phase literally causes the other, they rather make room (or "make time") for one another. They are equal segments of a process of change, so there is no reason to look upon one segment as the ultimate "source" of the other. Therefore the *Zhuangzi* has Confucius say the following (with Guo Xiang's commentary in italics):

> It is not because of life that what is dead is turned into what is alive. *Well, that which is dead is dead only because of change. It is not the case that what is alive would turn alive that which is dead.* It is not because of death that what is alive is turned into what is dead. *That which is alive is also alive because of change only.*[14]

What is alive is thoroughly alive. Once change takes place, once the positions turn around, once the reversal comes, there is something dead where earlier there was something alive. But it cannot be said that death kills life nor that life vivifies death. It is not a process of causation, it is a process of change. This process entails nothing like reincarnation. Change is complete: it is not the case that that which is now alive is later that which is then dead and may later be that which is alive again.

The allegory of Duke Niuai and his "illness of change" illustrates the "radical" character of the Daoist notion of change: Change turns a thing into something completely different.[15] There is no identity that is preserved throughout the process. Change dissolves a thing and puts something else in its place. Day replaces night, and today is not the "return" of yesterday—it's a radically different and separate day. In the course of change, only change prevails. The Daoist concept of change may be understood as an "ontology of process" as opposed to an "ontology of substance." The essential or primary element of an ontology of process is the process as such. Substantial being is only of secondary importance. Or rather, there are no "substances" in the strict sense of the word, because nothing "subsists," there is no permanent type of being beyond existence. The continuous process consists of phases of existence, not of substances. In an ontology of substance, entities like the "soul" are supposed to be of primary importance, while processual change is only secondary. On the basis of an ontology of substances, there is no absolute death to an "indivisible" soul—the soul does not change when the body dies. Here, the substantial being is privileged over types of processual existences.

Daoist texts like the *Zhuangzi* suggest an attitude of calm and easiness in the face of death. On the basis of an ontology of process, death does not bring about any substantial loss—since there is nothing substantial in the first place. Nothing of the person who is now alive will be dead, one will rather turn into something else. Therefore, one does not really die, because when one is dead, it is something else that is dead. Because change is total, one does not have to worry about what will happen to "oneself" after death. It will simply no longer be "oneself" who is dead.

The *Zhuangzi* and Guo Xiang often compare the relation between life and death to the relation between dreaming and being awake—the butterfly dream allegory is only one example of many. A person who is afraid of death is compared to someone who is afraid of falling asleep and dreaming. Such a dread is stupid and unnatural. It is also stupid and unnatural, from the perspective of Daoist philosophy, to value life more than death. One who is afraid of change has not yet understood the course of life and death—the course of the Way, the course of the Dao. To understand the course of the Dao means to understand the equal validity and authenticity of all segments of a process of change. The following passage from the *Zhuangzi* explains in detail the analogy between dreaming and being awake and living and being dead (the commentary by Guo Xiang is printed in italics):

> How do I know that a special liking for life is [justified and] not a delusion?

Life and death are a unit. Nevertheless to solely have a special liking for life means that [personal] desires and [the course of] change contradict each other. Thus one cannot yet be sure if this [special liking] might not really be a delusion.

How do I know that hating death is [justified and that death] is not just like [the condition of the] exile since childhood who will not know that he has returned home [if he comes home]?

"Exile since childhood" is a name for someone who has lost his former home at an early age. Such an exile will consequently be perfectly content wherever he is and will not even know if he returns to his hometown. How should one know that life is not such an "exile" and know that death is not such a "return," and therefore hate it?

Lady Li was the daughter of a frontier guard at Ai. When the kingdom of Jin first took her, her tears stained her dress; only when she came to the palace and shared the king's square couch and ate the flesh of hay-fed and grain-fed beasts did she begin to regret her tears.

This is what the change of feelings in a lifetime is like. On this day one does not know about that day. And how much more so when it comes to the change of life and death! How should it be possible that there is mutual knowledge [in the case of life and death]?

How do I know that the dead do not regret that they ever had an urge to live?

The character qi *means "to have an urge to."*

Who banquets in a dream wails and weeps at dawn, who wails and weeps in a dream at dawn goes out to hunt.

This is the change of events between being asleep and being awake. When the events change, the feeling becomes different. Therefore the respective comforts of life and death cannot be the same. Thus if one can be happily alive while being alive, one can be happily dead while being dead. Although life and death are different, they are one in both having their respective comforts. So why should one cling [to only one of them]?

While we dream we do not know that we are dreaming.

Looking at it from this perspective, one is not aware of being dead while one is dead and one then just does as it pleases.

In a dream we sometimes interpret a dream.

If someone dreams and in his dream interprets a dream, there is nothing by which to distinguish him from someone who is awake.

After we wake up, we know that we were dreaming.

What one meets [in each phase] is completely satisfying. So why should one while being alive worry about death?

There is also a great awakening after which we know that all that was a great dream.

> *The great awakened one is a sage. The great awakened one knows that all those who carry anxieties and concerns in themselves are not yet awake.*[16]

It is as groundless to esteem life as real and death as unreal as it is to believe that it feels better to be a awake than it does to be asleep. The exile since childhood has no knowledge about a home. He has forgotten the notion of home—the notion of belonging more to one place than to another. No matter where he is, he always feels fine. He has eradicated or forgotten the idea of an "authentic" home. There is no place which is more "real" for him than any other. To him, all places are equally valid. He has accepted change by forgetting any attachment to a "home." By forgetting a specific home, he is at home wherever he is. He can be perfectly at ease at any time at any place.

The little anecdote of Lady Li has the same Daoist "message": As long as one is afraid of change, one cannot be completely satisfied with one's presence. However, Lady Li's worries soon turn out to be unwarranted, and once she has totally accepted her new "home," once she has completely affirmed the new segment of change, she begins to cherish the specific comforts of her new presence. She is only ready to fully affirm her new presence when she forgets her former one. Her satisfaction depends on breaking with the past. This is also how one should face life and death. The change is always complete. One cannot measure the one phase by means of the other, and the attempt creates discontent. Being in one phase, one can only be happy and totally present if one forgets about the other. One will only be able to esteem the authenticity of each present phase by not worrying about what does not belong to it. Just as one cannot know how the fish are happy in the water, but know *that* they can be happy in the water by being happy on land, one also cannot know how one will be happy in death, but know *that* one can be happy in death by being happy in life.

Analogously, it is argued that one experiences dreams as being as real as one experiences being awake. This is illustrated by the fact that one may well dream about interpreting a dream—and in order to do this, one must obviously feel awake and real. In a case like this we indeed "explicitly" dream that we are awake and not asleep—and while we dream this we have no doubt that we are fully awake.

But what about the "great awakening" that is discussed at the end of the passage? How is this "great awakening" different from a "small awakening?" Zhuangzi and Guo Xiang had just stressed the full authenticity of all "small awakenings" and insisted that one should feel perfectly comfortable in each "small" phase of being, whether awake or asleep, alive or dead. What then is the need for a great awakening? In order to answer this literally "central" question, I would like to refer once more back to the butterfly dream allegory. Guo Xiang says:

> Well, the course of time does not stop for a moment, and today does not persist in what follows. Thus yesterday's dream changes into a today. How could it be different with the change between life and death!? Why should one let one's heart be made heavy by being moved back and forth between them? Being one, there is no knowledge of the other. Being a butterfly while dreaming is genuine. Relating this to human beings: when alive one does not know whether one may later actually have beautiful concubines. Only the stupid think they really know that life is something delightful and death is something to be sad about. That is what is called "never having heard of the changing of things."

This passage obviously parallels Guo Xiang's remarks on the cases of Lady Li and the exile since childhood. The latter shares Zhuang Zhou's situation in the butterfly dream: the exile was first at home, then somewhere else. When he finally returns, this return is not a return for him, because he no longer knows about his home. He has forgotten his home and so feels at home everywhere. Zhuang Zhou and the butterfly were likewise at home in all three stages described in the butterfly allegory because there was *no memory* that bridged the phases and diminished their respective presence. It is possible to interpret Zhuangzi's and Guo Xiang's philosophy of death in terms of the butterfly dream allegory—and it will also be possible to answer the question about the great awakening with its help.

The five philosophical motifs of the butterfly dream story—forgetting, the "Non-I," doubtlessness, barriers, and authenticity—are essential motifs of the Daoist philosophy of death: Forgetting about previous and future phases of change is the precondition for the affirmation of the presence of each phase. Death is just another segment within a process of change, and one will be perfectly at home in death by complete forgetfulness. This implies that there is no continuous "I" that persists in the course of life and death. Each phase has its respective "I," but no "I" subsists through the process of change. When "I" die, another "I" will be dead because of the barrier between life and death. One can be certain of the equal authenticity of the segments on each side of the barrier so one does not have to doubt what death will bring—it will certainly bring another form of authenticity.

The issue of the "great awakening" can be solved by taking into account the analogy between the above quoted reflections on death and the butterfly dream story. The distinction between the small and the great awakening parallels the distinction between Zhuang Zhou and Zhuangzi or Master Zhuang, the Daoist sage. The awake Zhuang Zhou exists within a segment of change, just like the butterfly in the dream. The small awakening is the awakening from such a "small dream," it is the change from one phase to the next. Within each phase, within each small dream and small waking, it is important to be fully absorbed within the phase, and each small segment is fully real. Life and death are such small segments of change and each step between the segments is a small awakening—or a small sleep. To newly awaken means to newly accept another stage in the process, to begin another life or death. The small awakening takes place in the "periphery" of change, and while in the periphery of change, while taking an "active" part in the process, it is best to be fully awake in one's presence. A small awakening is the full acceptance and integration of oneself in the present circumstances.

The great awakening is the awakening of the Daoist sage—it is his/her "enlightenment." It is the "ultimate" change from the present Zhuang Zhou to the nonpresent Master Zhuang. This awakening does not lead beyond life and death, but rather right to their center. A Daoist sage identifies him/herself not with the turning spokes of a wheel but with its unmoving hub. To be the pivot or center of change means to be identified with the whole process of change. This "zero-perspective" on the process of change is the Daoist sage's perspective on life and death, and the great awakening is the awakening to this perspective. As opposed to the small awakened who totally identifies him/herself with the present segment of change, with life or death, the sage identifies him/herself with neither of the specific segments, but with the whole process as such.

The Daoist sage is no longer a Zhuang Zhou and then a butterfly, one being alive and then one being dead, but reaches the "pivot of the Dao" (*dao shu*) and equally affirms both life and death. He/she views life and death as a ruler views the officials or as the heart views the organs. Without identifying with any specific elements of an organism—political or physical—he/she dwells in their midst and "controls" them. The great awakened sage does not "transcend" death, he/she accepts both death and life. The sage views the growth and decay of his/her physical body from the zero-perspective, and thus neither life nor death can harm him/her. The sage, as the *Zhuangzi* says, neither celebrates life nor laments death.[17] But the sage also does not lament life or celebrate death. The sage is indifferent because life and death are in-differently real to him/her. *The Daoist sage is no Jesus Christ and does not triumph over death, but affirms death in its lifelike or "life-equal" authenticity and validity.*

It is through this "attitude," through this great awakening to the zero-perspective on life and death that a Daoist sage becomes "immortal." The perishing of the body makes no difference to the sage for, as the *Zhuangzi* says, they "alter nothing in him/herself."[18] From the zero-perspective of the hub, the wheel always looks the same, no matter where the spokes are. Since the sage has no present "self" and no present identity or function, his/her own present body is his/her present periphery or environment. The periphery around the hub is in constant change—but from the perspective of the hub this change does not make a difference—it always looks the same. The same is true for the sage in regard to his/her body. The decay of the body causes no more worry to the sage than the withering of the plant worries the root. Death will replace life and life will again replace death, just like a withered plant replaces a flowering plant, which will itself be replaced by a new flowering plant. Thus, the sage is "without past and present" and enters "into the undying, unliving."[19] This is how philosophical Daoism reaches the goal of immortality, or the "Dao of not-dying," as the *Zhuangzi* puts it.[20] Unlike practical Daoism, this "Dao of not-dying" has nothing to do with physical longevity or permanence. The sage of philosophical Daoism avoids dying and living by emptying his/her self both physically and "spiritually." In his/her periphery times and seasons change, thoughts come and go, the body grows and shrinks, and in winter it will feel cold, and in summer it will feel hot, but because the sage identifies with the empty center of these processes, he/she affirms the course of events and lets them happen without being touched.

An impressive illustration of the Daoist sage's attitude towards life and death is Mengsun Cai, the "artist of mourning," who is introduced in the *Zhuangzi*. Mengsun Cai cries when it is time for crying, but he sheds no tears, because his heart is empty and cannot be harmed by feelings. The story about Mengsun Cai is told in the context of a dialogue between Confucius and his disciple Yan Hui. In this dialogue Confucius is not only presented as an expert on mourning rites and thus as a good Confucian, but, more importantly, also as a good Daoist, because he is able to explain how and why Mengsun Cai is a true sage who surpasses even Confucius himself in the art of mourning. Mengsun Cai knows how to mourn without mourning. The dialogue between Confucius and Yan Hui once more entails all the motifs of Daoist death philosophy that were discussed in relation to the butterfly dream allegory. In English translation it reads (with Guo Xiang's commentary in italics):

> Yan Hui asked Confucius: "Mengsun Cai wailed when his mother died but did not shed a tear. At the center, his heart did not mourn. Conducting the funeral, he did not grieve. In spite of this threefold incorrectness, he is renowned as the best of mourners throughout the state of Lu. This is certainly a case of someone winning a name without possessing the substance. I am utterly amazed at it." *In the state of Lu, [people] observed Mengsun Cai's following of the rites, whereas Yan Hui investigated Mengsun Cai's heart.*
>
> Confucius said: "Mengsun Cai has exhaustively grasped the matter, he has taken a step beyond [mere] knowledge [of the rites]. *He has exhaustively grasped the pattern of life and death. He is someone who inwardly and outwardly responds appropriately and moves in accord with the motions of heaven; he is not someone who is [merely] a companion of knowledge [of rules].* He [had tried] to pick only [one of the phases death and life as real] but did not succeed. *He picked either life or death and could not see any difference [of reality]. [Their change] was [to him] just like the sequence of the four seasons spring and fall, winter and summer.* When he just had picked one [phase], Mengsun Cai either did not know [in the case he had picked life] how it had come to life, or he did not know [in the case he had picked death] how it had come to die. *By having picked one, he could not [see a difference of reality]. Therefore there was no discontent [with any of the*

phases]. Because there was no discontent [with any of the phases], he com-
plied with [the change of] life and death without having his mind dis-
turbed by it. It was self-change. Neither did he know what had
preceded, nor did he know what would follow. *However he met it, he*
was content. If he had just changed into something—*he did not resist*
change—on what should he rely in regard to [the phases of] change
which he did not know about? *Life and death give way to each other in*
turn and form a unit in change. Thus in the presence [of one phase] one
forgets what one had known [in the other phase]. How can one have long-
range worries which rely on something one does not yet know? At the state
of being changed, how would he know about the state of not being
changed? At the state of not being changed, how would he know
about the state of being changed? *While having changed into being*
alive, does one know about the time in which one was not yet alive? While
one was not yet changed and dead, did one know about what would come
after being dead? Thus there is nothing to avoid and nothing to go after,
and one can completely go with the course of change. May not you and
I presently be within a dream out of which we have not yet awakened?
Well, life and death are just like being awake and in a dream. When one
is dreaming, one believes oneself to be awake. Thus there is nothing to
prove that one is not dreaming when [one feels] awake. If there is noth-
ing to prove that one is not dreaming when [one feels] awake, then there
is also nothing to prove that one is not dead when [one feels] alive.
Neither in life nor in death, neither in a dream nor while awake, does
one know in which [phase] one is. And therefore whichever presence one
meets, one can always be fully self-content in it. How is it that while
[people] are here [they] worry about [being] there? To him [Mengsun
Cai] there are shapes which surprisingly alter, but this does not harm
his heart. *He simply takes change as a surprising alteration of shape.*
Therefore his heart is unharmed by [the change] of life and death. To
him there is a new construction of a hut at a new morning, but he is
not emotionally stirred by death. *He takes the changing of the body as*
a new construction of a hut on a new day. Emotionally, he does not take
it as dying. Mengsun is very much awake. When the others wail he
wails too. This is due to his nature. *Well, one who is constantly awake*
does not resist the proceedings [of nature]. Thus it is correct that he wails
when the others wail. It is by this nature of his that he [acts so] appro-
priately. Besides, while we are here together, we take ourselves to be
just ourselves. *Well, in [the course of] the change of life and death we all*
take ourselves to be ourselves. If we always take ourselves to be genuine,
how should this "ourselves" ever be lost? And if this "ourselves" is not yet
lost, why should we worry? Because he is without resistance, [Mengsun
Cai] wails when the others wail. Because he is without worries, he wails

without grief. How would we invariably know what we mean when we take us to be ourselves? *We never do not take us to be ourselves. Thus the outer and the inner are mysteriously united and the past and the present are in complete continuity. With change there is something new daily. How should one know where we "ourselves" are?* In your dream, for instance, you become a bird, and you fly away in the sky. Or in your dream, you become a fish, and you plunge into the deep. *This says that wherever one goes one can be fully self-content.* Thus there is no telling whether the one who speaks now is awake or dreaming. *At the time of a dream, one takes oneself to be awake. So how can one know that the present is not a dream—or that it is not being awake? The [course of] change of dreaming and being awake can go anywhere. Thus in [the course of] the change of life and death, there is no [phase of] time which gives sufficient [reason] for misery.* If one is totally in accord with events, it will not come about that one laughs [out of happiness]. If one should laugh [out of happiness], it will not come about that one [spontaneously] gives way to the shift. *By being in total accord with events, one forgets about being in accord. Therefore it will not come about that one laughs [out of happiness]. The word "shift" is meant in the sense of an alteration movement. Well, in order to wail according to the [mourning] rites, the heart has to grieve. In order to laugh [out of happiness], one has to be joyful. But when grief and joy are within one's bosom, then one cannot be in accord with the alteration movement. Now, Mengsun is continuously in accord [with the course of events]. Therefore he wails without grief and completely goes with the course of change.* [Mengsun Cai] had been content in giving way to the shift and went with change. Then he entered into the solitary spot and formed the unity with heaven. *[Mengsun Cai] had been content within the alteration movement and completely went with the course of change. Then he consequently entered into the still and solitary spot and formed the unity with heaven. What is conveyed [in the text passages] from here up to the [the case] of Zisi is the same, only the funerals are different. Therefore, there is this contrast between singing [in the cases above] and [Mengsun Cai's] wailing.*[21]

The last two sentences of Guo Xiang's impressive commentary relate back to other stories about dying and funerals in the *Zhuangzi.* Only a few lines before this dialogue, there is another between Confucius and one of his disciples about the behavior of two Daoist masters who laugh and sing at the occasion of the death of their closest companion. Guo Xiang points out that the singing Daoists and the wailing Mengsun Cai share the same attitude towards life and death—although they act quite contrary to each other. Daoist sages view life and death as equally authentic segments within the process of change. Each segment of change goes along with a notion of an "I" or an "ourselves." And with each disappearance of a segment, such an "I" or such an "ourselves" disappears. However, since each disappearance is followed by a new appearance, there will be a new "I" that replaces the old one—just like a newly built hut on a new day. Therefore the death of an "I" is nothing sad; there is no reason to be worried about the course of events. The future "I" will be different from the past, but not less real or deficient in being. Death is no loss—it is just a step forward. Because there is nothing sad about death, a Daoist sage can sing at a funeral—or wail without feeling grief. From the perspective of the Daoist sage, dying is no more sad than falling asleep or waking up.

Another reason for not devaluating death—and therefore for not being emotionally disturbed by it—is that we cannot even know if we are presently dead or alive. The *Zhuangzi* and Guo Xiang argue that because we feel perfectly awake when we have a "lively" dream, we cannot know for certain if we are not dreaming while we suppose that we are awake and reading the *Zhuangzi*. Analogously, while we surely feel perfectly alive right now while reading this text, we may nevertheless be actually dead. We have no proof that we are now in a phase of existence that is more real than the preceding or the following one. The only precondition for fully realizing the authenticity of the present is to realize the radical separation between the segments of change. There is no continuous "ourselves" in the course of life and death—and thus there is no memory and knowledge—in either direction of time. From the perspective of the Daoist sage, there can hardly be anything more foolish then the attempt to find out what the "I" was in a previous life or what will come of "myself" in a future death. Such memory or knowledge has no foundation and will only amount to a "worry" that detaches the present I from its presence. The Daoist sage does *not* believe in the reincarnation of an I.

Because the Daoist sage does not resist the course of events, he/she also does not resist social customs. Mengsun Cai, the artist of mourning, lives in the state of Lu—the state of Confucius. Confucianism cultivated the rites and the human emotions that go along with these ceremonies. The Confucians mourn when its time to mourn—that is, at the time of death. Because Mengsun Cai does not resist, he also will mourn when it is time to mourn. As a man of Lu, he wails with all the others who wail for his mother. But the ceremonies cannot touch Mengsun Cai's heart. His heart is a Daoist sage's heart, and this heart is empty. It cannot be saddened by the process of change.

The Daoist friends mentioned earlier in the *Zhuangzi* laughed and sang at the funeral of one of their friends because neither of them, including the deceased, thought death to be worse than life. Mengsun Cai wailed at his mother's funeral, because he does not resist the customs of Lu—though he felt no more sorrow than the Daoist friends. In both dialogues, Confucius explains the Daoist sage's "mindset" to his disciples and acknowledges it to be "wiser" or rather more in accord with the Dao than the Confucian cultivation of emotions and behavior, and their practice of morality and rites. Zhuangzi's Confucius admits that the Confucian mourning of the dead is not as sagely as the Daoist elimination of feelings. Only the Daoist emotional indifference does justice to the natural in-difference of life and death.

The Daoist friends who sang when one of their companions died asked each other:

> Who is able to have emptiness as the head, life as the spine, death as the rump? Who knows that life and death, persistence and decline are all one body? With such a person we will be friends! [22]

These Daoist sages would surely have welcomed Mengsun Cai into their "club." Mengsun Cai had, "at the center," emptied his heart of feelings, and that is quite the same as having "emptiness as the head." To empty one's heart of feelings and thus to have emptiness as one's head is to take on the zero-perspective. To attain this state is described as a sort of development—it is the step from the small awakening to the great awakening. This step is made by an identification with presence. Zhuang Zhou had been fully "himself" and the butterfly was likewise "itself." Mengsun Cai had proceeded with the course of change and picking the different phases of life and death found them equally real. He had always been fully "himself" in each stage, he "had been content in giving way to the shift and went with change." But at the very end of his story, he "leaps" into Daoist sagacity, into the hub of the wheel of life and death. The text says: "Then he entered into the solitary spot and formed the unity with heaven." At this stage, Mengsun Cai has given up any present identity and thus he can identify with the whole process of change: he has "life as the spine, death as the rump." At this second stage he is no longer fully content within either life or death, but has "greatly awakened" from both.

Daoist practice aimed at transforming the physical body into an organism structured according to the pattern of the Dao. Philosophical Daoism related to the same pattern, but does not try to transform the body into a microcosmic whole. It rather pursues an emptying of the mind that allows for an unemotional affirmation of both life and death. In the face of death, the greatest and absolute threat, Daoist philosophy tries to attain utmost indifference. But this attitude is not "heroic"—there is no defiance of death on behalf of the Daoist sage, he/she is no "braveheart." The Daoist sage is unafraid of death because he/she has forgotten all anxiety about it. This total forgetfulness has neutralized the sage and put him/her in a position of feeling neither "merely" dead nor "merely" alive, neither "just" mortal nor "just" living. The Daoist sage leaps into the midst of life and death—or as the *Zhuangzi* puts it: "For these men of old, there was change externally and no change internally."[23]

4. Time

Daoist concepts of time revolve around two ideals: the ideal of permanence and the ideal of "the right moment." The ideal of the right moment entails the concepts of acting at the right time and being at the right place at the right time. These concepts are connected with the concept of a correct temporal sequence of events such as, for instance, the cycle of the four seasons or of day and night. Life and death—as discussed in the preceding chapter—are also conceived of as temporal segments within a continuous and regular course of time. The sequence of segments that have to be present at the right time make up the complete and permanent whole. The ideals of permanence and the right moment belong together. Fulfilling the ideal of the right moment (for each time segment) is the precondition for fulfilling the ideal of permanence (of the course of time consisting of these segments). The continuity of the whole process of time depends on the temporal limitation, on the temporary nature of its constitutive elements. Only the course of temporal change is permanent, while the temporal phases within this course are impermanent.

In the *Daodejing* the ideal of permanence is of outstanding importance. Here, it is directly applied to the art of government—the Daoist sage ruler is supposed to lend permanence to the political body. The "other side" of this ideal is the fear of transitoriness—a fear that Daoists tried to overcome. While Daoist practitioners invented all kinds of means to protect themselves against the transitoriness of the physical body, the *Daodejing* alludes to a host of political strategies to make the state more permanent—and such strategies were badly needed in the time of the "Warring States" in which each state more or less continuously threatened the existence of the others. Chapter 23 in the *Daodejing* expresses this fear of transitoriness:

> A whirlwind does not last a morning.
> A downpour does not last a day.
> Who is acting in these cases?
>> Heaven and earth—
>> but even these can't make them last.
> How then, should man be able to?

Even certain "actions" of nature—such as whirlwinds and downpour—are unable to last and are obviously a momentary and destructive waste of power rather than a durable and productive use of energy. If even nature sometimes fails to bring about duration—how much more is this task for the most fragile of the three cosmic realms—man (next to heaven and earth). Daoist philosophy tries to provide mankind with a pattern of permanence to compensate for the fear of transitoriness. Within this pattern, impermanence is not eliminated but integrated into an encompassing duration. In a certain sense, Daoist permanence represents the threefold Hegelian *Aufhebung*[24] of impermanence: the continuity of the process of the Way (Dao) "preserves" the impermanence of the time segments—nothing will last as such—but it also "raises" them so that they can be regarded as elements of a process of duration, and thus the initial impermanence is actually "abolished."

The very first sentence of the *Daodejing* discusses in a typically paradoxical fashion the issue of permanence:

> As to a Dao—
>> if it can be specified as a Dao,
>> it is not a permanent Dao.

The Dao as a structure of permanence is constituted by specific, definite, and temporally limited phases, but because these phases are complementary *opposites*, the Dao itself is not specific and definite. Paradoxically, the permanent is composed of impermanent elements, and the indefinite and unlimited is composed of definite and limited segments. The cyclic process of the year cannot be identified with or characterized by any definite and limited season—and therefore the "Way" of the year is not a specific way although it consists of specific time segments. The specific elements of time are not permanent, while the permanent course of time is not specific.

In the political realm, as well as in the "cosmic" cycle of the year, it is of the utmost importance that everything happens at the right time. If the seasons do not come at the right time, if the winters are not cold and if the summers are not hot, then natural disasters will result. Analogously, if people do not act in accordance with the course of time—if they do not sow and harvest at the appropriate time, for instance, or if administrative orders are issued in an untimely way—there will be a social crisis. Therefore, the ruler, above all, has to supervise the timeliness of his subjects' activities. He who does not himself act has to observe that all actions are done when it is the time to do them. Thus chapter 8 of the *Daodejing* says about the Daoist sage ruler:

In having actions performed,
   His goodness lies in timeliness.

If all tasks are fulfilled at the right time, events will naturally unfold in a productive and efficient way. Thus, not only will nature and society proceed constantly and permanently, not only will the state last, but also at every moment of the process everything will be perfectly present. Nothing will occur too late or too early, nothing of yesterday or tomorrow will intermingle with today's business. There will be no violations of the barriers of time, and thus, in a strict sense there is neither a past nor a future, but only presence. Guo Xiang's commentary on the butterfly dream allegory illustrated how a lingering on of the past (remembrance of earlier stages of existence) or anticipations of the future (worries about future stages of existence—such as death) will irritate and eventually spoil the enjoyment of pure presence. One who dwells on what is gone may develop a nostalgia and may be unable—like Lady Li when she arrived at the king's court—to appreciate the here and now. Similarly, the one who is anxious about what will come cannot be fully content in his or her momentary reality. Such mental transgressions of the barriers of presence violate the Daoist ideal of the right moment. The happiness and self-sufficiency of the butterfly in the dream are dependent upon the complete forgetting of the past and future Zhuang Zhou. Authenticity of existence is directly connected with the immediate experience of time, with the absorption in pure presence. If one leaps intellectually into the future or into the past, one loses the immediacy of the present and this harms one's integration into the flow of time. To introduce the past or the future into the present means to produce temporal friction.

The transgression of presence is dangerous. It will not only reduce the enjoyment of full presence—one won't be as happy as the fish in the river Hao—but it also puts the harmonious course of time at risk. To overstep the limits of time is analogous to overstepping the limits of one's profession and can be looked upon as a "crime" similar to that of the royal keeper of the hat. In a perfectly ordered, harmonious, and "natural" society people will not only stick to their specific tasks, but also perform their tasks only at the correct time.

The Daoist course of time is therefore a chain of presence—it is not a continuous transformation of future into past. Influential Western conceptions of time, for example, that of St. Augustine, have diminished presence to an infinitely small moment in between long stretches of past and future. As opposed to such devaluations of presence, the Daoist conception of time is based on a continuous sequence of *extended* phases of presence. From a Daoist point of view, the endless—and "beginningless"—course of time consists of mutually replacing temporal "nows."

The sequence of extended phases of presence corresponds to the turning of the spokes within a wheel. But what about the hub? While the wheel, as a kind of *perpetuum mobile*, represents the continuous process of the Dao, the hub represents the literally "timeless" center of timely change. Like the wheel, time is also believed to turn around a nonturning center. Again, it is up to the Daoist sage to identify him/herself not with the changing segments of presence, but with the pivot that keeps the process of time in proper balance. The Daoist sage has to get to the heart of time. In the *Zhuangzi* it is said (with Guo Xiang's commentary in italics):

> Ranxiang got to the center of the circle and brought about completion by accordance.
>
> *Ranxiang was a sage ruler in antiquity. He dwelled in emptiness and was in accord with [the course of] things. The [course of] things came by themselves to completion.*
>
> [In accordance] with the [course of] things he had no beginning and no end, no moment, no time.
>
> *Instantly, he went on [in] complete [accordance] with [the course of] things.*
>
> The one who changes daily with [the course of] things is the single one who does not change.
>
> *Daily, he changes with [the course of] things. Therefore he is permanently without an I. Because he is permanently without an I, he permanently does not change.*[25]

The sage ruler Ranxiang is a true Daoist. He is a sage of time, because he "got to the center of the circle" and thus can be in accordance with the whole course of time. Because he is without the "three times" (*san shi*)—that is to say without past, present, and future—as the subcommentary to the above passage by Guo Qingfan (1844–1896 CE) states,[26] he completes the cycle of time by "adding" the timeless center to it. "Instantly," he goes along with time—like the hub goes along with the wheel. Each day he is within time, but he does not change with it. Whereas all things have their time, whereas all things have their presence, he accompanies their course without having a specific and definite time segment for himself. He resembles the root of a tree: The root does not change its appearance—it cannot be seen—while the tree changes drastically in the course of the seasons. Ranxiang is at the center of the temporal circle, and this center is needed to make the circle run smoothly.

Every specific time phase, every moment of presence, is tied to an I. These "I's" all have a beginning and an end, they all come and go. While awake, there is an I of Zhuang Zhou; while asleep, it is replaced by an I of a butterfly. The "I's" change with time. Only one without an I—only one with an empty heart—does not change. Ranxiang does not change because he is at the center of the circle. But if one takes on the perspective of the whole process of time, it can also be said that Ranxiang is in accord with the continuous flow of time. Thus, Ranxiang is both without and never apart from time.

The timeless Daoist sage does not take anything away from the authenticity of the temporal. Unlike Western conceptions of eternity, which tend to devaluate all that is merely temporal, the Daoist concept of timelessness affirms the realm of temporality and of passing time. Just as the sage affirms both life and death, the sage also affirms the course of time. While he/she is without presence, without beginning and end, he/she still always "goes on in accord with the course of things." He/she is the nonpresence that always accompanies the sequence of presence.

While the Daoist sage is timeless within time, he/she is well aware of change. The following (strictly parallel structured) passage from the *Zhuangzi* describes what the unfolding of the course of time looks like when seen from the zero-perspective of the sage:

> Well, regarding the realm of things,
>> measures have no base,
>> [the course of] time has no stop,
>> distinctions have no constancy,
>> ending and beginning have no ground.
> Therefore,
>> —if one wisely looks into far and near,
>>> one will neither belittle the smaller nor make much of the greater,
>>> knowing that [in the realm of things] measures have no base.
>> —if one clearly comprehends past and present,
>>> one will neither be gloomy because of the long-timed nor worry because of the short-timed,
>>> knowing that [in the realm of things the course of] time has no stop.
>> —if one investigates the full and the empty,
>>> one will neither be pleased by winning nor saddened by losing,
>>> knowing that [in the realm of things] distinctions have no constancy.
>> —if one is clear-sighted about the plain path,
>>> one will neither rejoice in being alive nor think it calamity to die,
>>> knowing that [in the realm of things] ending and beginning have no ground.[27]

In the world of events and actions, in the world of life and death, constant change takes place: "[the course of] time has no stop." Everything that is distinct from other things has its time and is distinct by having its time. It will be replaced once its time runs out and the time of another thing comes. Thus neither loss nor gain, neither beginning nor end are "finite." Every gain is a loss for something else and will, in turn, turn into a loss for another's gain. According to the Daoist rule of reversal, every beginning will turn into an end, and every end is also a beginning.

From the zero-perspective of the Daoist sage the respective phases or time segments are in-differently valid. In its own time, the small and the short-timed is neither small nor short-timed. It only looks small or short-timed if it is seem from the perspective of the great or long-timed. Likewise, the time of death only looks frightening and less real if it is seen from the perspective of life. In the world of things and time, it is important not to overstep the distinctions of time. One should not compare one's time with another. Only if one stays fully within one's time, can one be totally *present*. Seen strictly from within, the short is not short and the long is not long.

For the Daoist sage all of these "perspectives from within" are equally real and equally limited. Everything has its respective time—and this is fine. Only the sage "has no time"—and thus has all the time. He/she identifies him/herself with the course of time. He/she has no specific presence, no perspective from within a certain time, no "I," and thus he/she with clear sight watches on while the near and the far, the present and the past, the empty and the full replace each other on the "plain path" of time.

Given the structure of this concept of time, the problem of an ultimate beginning of time or of the creation of time—which was an important issue in traditional Western philosophy—cannot arise. Beginning and end only exist for the segments within the always moving course of time. Phases come and go, but time remains. The "plain path" of time has neither beginning nor end—these are "categories" within time, but not of time itself. The course of time turns like a wheel-shaped *perpetuum mobile*—without a start and a stop. In the monistically closed scenario of time there is nothing that transcends time, *there is no notion of eternity that functions like a kind of "coat" of time*. Things and events constitute the course of time through change and replacement, and the Daoist sage is integrated into this flow. He/she does not exclude him/herself from change but dissolves him/herself into it. He/she is within change, not above it. Unlike in Christianity, for instance, the timelessness of the sage is not an act of overcoming time and transitoriness; it is not a devaluation of time, but an affirmation of the full reality and authenticity of passing time.

The Daoist sage does not create time; he rather vanishes in the midst of its passing. In the *Zhuangzi* (with the commentary by Guo Xiang in italics), the cultivation of this attitude is described as a three-step process:

> There are those for whom there is a beginning.
> *If there is a beginning [for them], there is also an end.*
> There are those for whom having a beginning has not yet begun.
> *This says that when there is neither beginning nor end, life and death are taken as a unity.*
> There are those for whom [even] the not yet beginning of having a beginning has not yet begun.
> *Well, to take life and death as a unity is not as good as allowing for the equal validity of these phases just by themselves without taking them as a unity. This is to even forget their unity.*[28]

Those who have a beginning and who believe that their existence goes back to a starting point necessarily exist within a segment of time. Such beings or people can be totally happy and self-content in their respective presence, and if so, they will experience their presence as fully authentic. But certainly their "I" will be replaced by another "I" with the change of time. This change will be the end of their existence. If one relates oneself to a beginning, then one settles one's "I" within a segment of time and exposes it to transitoriness and termination. Every "I" is a specific and distinct "I," and therefore it will have its own history—its own distinct realm within the course of time. Every "I" necessarily has its own biography, and by having a biography it has a beginning and an end. If one claims an "individual" place in time, one also inevitably claims an individual beginning and an individual end. The "I" is intrinsically connected with a beginning and an end.

If one does not begin by identifying oneself with a beginning in time, then one can somehow escape the limitations of time—but one pays the price of losing one's identity. If one no longer identifies oneself with an "I," one no longer cares about the mortality of this "I" and does not "mind" that this "I" is going to be replaced by another in time. From this perspective life and death form a unity, so one cannot suppose that the change between them can be traced back to an ultimate beginning—which would make one phase the ultimate "cause" of the other. One does not know where one's "I" will go and where it came from. The mourning artist Mengsun Cai had forgotten about his origins and his prospects and thus about his beginning and end. The emptying of the "I" enables the Daoist sage to enter the timeless center in between the phases of time. The sage does not leave time behind and enter an eternity with his/her pure but all the more individual "soul," he/she rather leaves the realm of beginning and end by leaving behind anything that resembles an individual soul.

The third step described in the above passage does not lead further beyond the timeless center of time, but rather explains the consequences of reaching this point. Where there is no "I" and no beginning and end, there cannot even be something that is taken as a unity. Nothing can be taken as anything. The total forgetfulness of the "I" goes along with a total forgetfulness of time. If there is perfect forgetting, even the unity will be forgotten. This last step may be paralleled to the "negative method" of philosophy suggested by the modern Chinese philosopher Feng Youlan.[29] Feng Youlan, relating back to ancient Daoism, acknowledged the methodological problems connected to the paradoxical and absurd philosophy of total forgetfulness: If it is a philosophy of absolute forgetting—how can one talk and think about it? In this last stage, a philosopher in the style of Zhuangzi or Feng Youlan must admit that one cannot even speak about any unity of, for instance, life and death, or about the Dao. The sage who empties his/her heart of an "I" and of time will be a nonspeaking philosopher. He/she will not even talk or think about the fact that not having a beginning did not yet begin for him/her—he/she will not even begin *this* discourse.

5. Nature

In his early-twentieth-century masterpiece, *La Pensée Chinoise* (Chinese Thought), the French Sinologist Marcel Granet presented an impressive in-depth analysis of ancient Chinese thought. This outstanding study on the philosophy of ancient China con-

tains a detailed examination of the concept of the Dao. My own
attempts to elucidate the Dao connect specifically to a passage
where Granet explains (without mentioning Daoism or chapter 11
of the *Daodejing*) the origin and structure of the notion of the
Dao on the basis of "the image of a pivot and a circulation."[30]
Granet traces the Chinese term *dao* back to the name for a *gnomon*, a long wooden pole erected at the center of the world that
reaches up into the sky. The function of this gnomon in ancient
China is described by Marcel Granet as follows:

> When the sovereigns founded a capital or determined the crossing of
> the roads on which the tributes of the four directions would be
> brought to them, they had to observe the play of shadow and light (of
> Yin and Yang) and to plant a gnomon. In their political mysticism, the
> Chinese always maintained the principle according to which in the
> capital of a perfect ruler the gnomon was not supposed to cast any
> shadow at midsummer's midday. Even more instructive are the myths.
> At the very center of the universe—where the perfect capital was sup-
> posed to be located—there stands a marvelous tree which connects
> the Nine Sources with the Nine Skies; it connects the foundation of
> the world with its ridge. *It is called the Erected Tree (jian mu), and it
> is said that nothing which is in its vicinity* and is perfectly upright *can
> cast a shadow.* Also, nothing will produce an echo. By a synthesis
> (which is perfect, because it results from hierogamy) all contrasts and
> all alternations, all attributes, and all signs are absorbed by the central
> Unity.[31]

This paradigmatic image of the structure of the cosmos or of
the whole of "nature" corresponds to the Daoist image of the Dao
as a perfect scenario. At the center of the world is the *Erected Tree*,
a gnomon that serves as the pivot of the circulation of nature. This
gnomon is both at the center of space (at the point where the
crossroads of the four directions meet) and at the center of time
(at the center of the year it casts no shadow[32])—it is the hub of the
cosmic wheel. The political sovereign finds and occupies this spot.
By marking and taking on the position of the center, the sovereign
demonstrates that he is "in control" (which is, of course, a control
without an active control) of the Dao. The positioning of the gnomon demonstrates not only the assuming of political power but
also the sovereign's claim to be at the center of the cosmos, of time
and space. The positioning and installation of the pivot at the cen-

ter unite the cultural and natural world. This unity then syntheti-
cally unites all divergent "contrasts and all alternations, all attrib-
utes, and all signs." The whole "positive" world of actions and
events, of the segments of space and time, come together at the
gnomon—and only is this space perfectly empty of everything: it
casts no shadow, it has no echo, it is without shape and sound, and
it absorbs all characteristics and is not subject to change and alternation. The ancient Chinese conception of nature and of the
macrocosmic world, as described by Granet, share their structure
with the Daoist conceptions of the state, the body, and time.

The erection of the gnomon results from the observation of the
rhythm of Yin and Yang, that is of the rhythm of light and shadow,
of brightness and darkness. An observation of the rhythm of nature
gives rise to the establishment of its center. The "observation" of
nature is thus not the observation of something external—it is the
observation of the ongoing scenario of which the observer is a
part. This observation does not lead—as in modern science—to
the establishment of static rules or laws, but rather to the self-posi-
tioning of the observer within the dynamic scenario. It resembles
the observation of a dance in order to participate in it—not in
order to note down an analysis of its steps. The observer does not
distance him/herself from the observed, but integrates him/her-
self into it. A Daoist sage is a perfect observer of the rhythm of
nature, but his/her perfect observation is not that of a modern
expert in the natural sciences.

The perfect perspective for the perfect observer of the rhythm
of nature is, of course, the zero-perspective. The Daoist sage
resembles the perfect ruler described by Granet in that he/she
manifests the "synthesis" of the course of nature by positioning
him/herself at its center. Therefore, the *Zhuangzi* literally calls
the position of the sage not only the "pivot of the Dao" (*dao shu*)
and the "center of the circle" (*huan zhong*), but also states—in the
very same passage—that the sage "illuminates [the world] from
[the perspective of] heaven" (*zhao zhi yu tian*).[33] The term for
"heaven" (*tian*) can also be translated as "nature." The perspective of the sage is the perspective of the gnomon, of the position
around which space and time circulate. Just as the hub can be
identified with the whole wheel, the gnomon as the center of the
rhythm of nature can be identified with that whole rhythm of
nature. The zero-perspective is also the all-perspective. By taking

on the perspective of "heaven" or "nature," the sage incorporates him/herself into nature. The sage thus affirms nature and performs its synthesis.

The rhythm of nature is constituted by complementary elements, such as shadow and light, night and day, and hot and cold. In Marcel Granet's terminology, Yin and Yang are the "main rubrics" (*rubriques maitresses*) or categories that structure the rhythm of nature.[34] Ancient Chinese philosophy was, generally speaking, very fond of classifications. Everything in the world—in nature or in society—could be grouped into complementary categories of a functional scenario. Day and night, brightness and darkness, the sun and the moon, for instance, were natural phenomena classified as corresponding to the "main rubrics" Yang and Yin. This "logic of rubrics" was elaborated by ancient Chinese philosophers, including the Daoists, into a complex network of classifications. The two main rubrics Yin and Yang were soon expanded into the system of the so-called "five phases" (*wu xing*: wood, fire, earth, metal, water), which in turn gave rise to immensely manifold taxonomical systems. Practically all realms of nature and culture could be described in this way: medicine and warfare, geography and ritual, astronomy and literature could be, for example, categorized and explained with the help of classificatory models.

Like ancient philosophy in general, Daoism looked upon nature as a complex process that unfolds according to the patterns of Yin and Yang. Nature was conceived of as a rhythmic sequence of segments and phases. The most basic expression of this conception is found in the *Great Commentary* (*Dazhuan*) to the *Book of Changes* (*Yijing*)—a text that recent Chinese research tries to identify more with classical Daoism than, as it was "traditionally" the case, with classical Confucianism.[35] The *Great Commentary* states: "One Yin, one Yang: this is called Dao." (*yi yin yi yang, zhi wei dao*).[36] Marcel Granet quite rightly remarks on this crucial formula: "The Dao is not the sum but the regulator (I do not say: law) of their alternation."[37] One may then translate the same phrase as: "One time Yin and one time Yang—this is called [the rhythm] of Dao." This general concept of nature meant in a more specifically Daoist context that the Dao is the regulator of nature as a rhythmic process, and the Daoist sage has to identify him/herself with the Dao.

"Heaven," or nature (*tian*), is for ancient Daoist philosophers a term that designates the whole scenario of cosmic and social functioning, the course of time and the pattern of space. The course of nature is the course of the Dao. Daoist practice aims at shaping oneself according to the pattern of this course, at becoming isomorphic with its pattern. By emptying his/her heart, the Daoist sage establishes it as his/her gnomon, so to speak. At his/her heart, at the center of his/her body and mind, the Daoist sage performs the "synthesis" of nature. Like the perfect sovereign, the Daoist sage aims at occupying or positioning him/herself at the center of nature. But for the Daoist sage this is not a political action, it is rather a process of "philosophical" cultivation.

If one defines "nature" as the whole cosmic functioning, then the ancient Chinese term *tian*—literally meaning "sky"—can surely be translated in many Daoist texts, especially in the *Zhuangzi*, as "nature." *Tian* often designates not only the "celestial" realm, but, as a *pars pro toto* figure of speech, all "natural" processes. If one, however, defines "nature" not so much as the sum of cosmic events, but rather as that which is as it was "born," as that which has not been subject to any "artificial" modification or alteration, as "authentic" and "unspoiled," then another Daoist term translates "nature" better than *tian*. If one understands "natural" in the sense of "pure" and "innate," then *ziran* designates Daoist "nature." *Ziran* means the "self-so" state of a thing, an event, or an action.

Considering the conception of the Dao as a *perpetuum mobile*, the notion of *ziran* expresses the complete "naturalness" of the Dao. Like a *perpetuum mobile*, the Dao is without any external input or modification, an ideal process that functions both by itself and permanently since it is not dependent on any outside cause. In the frictionless scenario, be it the wheel, the perfect state, or the immortal body, whatever happens, happens "naturally." In this sense, *ziran* designates the "own course" of a perfectly structured process. A process that runs smoothly without obstruction or loss of energy runs "self-so." Chapter 25 of the *Daodejing* expresses this perfectly "natural" character of the Dao in a paradigmatic way:

> I do not know its name.
> It is called Dao.
> If I was forced to name it,
>   I would say "Greatness."

"Greatness" means "to proceed."
"To proceed" means "distance."
"Distance" means "return."

The Dao is great.
Heaven is great.
The earth is great.
The king is also great.
In the land there are four greats—
     and the king positions himself where they are one.
Man follows the earth as a rule.
The earth follows heaven as a rule.
Heaven follows the Dao as a rule.
The Dao follows its "own course" [*ziran*] as a rule.

This passage begins with a description of the circularity of the process of the Dao: the Dao proceeds into the distance, but this proceeding is not a straight movement, it is a constant turn—thus the movement of the Dao forms a circle. In the second "verse" the (circular) movement of the Dao is portrayed as its "own course," its "self-so" (*ziran*). This movement is its own rule, and it is also the rule of the circulation of the celestial bodies. In turn this is the model for the movement of the earth and its seasons, which structures the circular process of human activities in an agrarian society. The "natural" (*ziran*) way in which the Dao moves, namely the circular motion, is the rule for all of nature, beginning with heaven (*tian*). Nature (*tian*) is a natural (*ziran*) process, and because it is so perfectly natural, nature has no external mover. The Dao simply follows its own course as does nature. The only rule of nature is its very own. The Daoist concept of nature is a concept of perfect immanence, of a perfectly closed (like a circle) monistic pattern of efficiency. It is a concept of *autopoiesis* or self-generation and self-production. The course of nature is neither initiated nor dependent on any transcendent "maker" or "creator." Nature is so natural because it creates, makes and continues itself. This is the "greatness" of the Dao.

6. Artisanship and Art

Daoist aesthetics and art are intrinsically connected with Daoist conceptions of artisanship. The Daoist piece of art is not different in nature from a Daoist piece of craftsmanship—both are modeled on the great "natural" artisanship of the Dao. Likewise, the Daoist artist and the Daoist craftsman are variations of the Daoist sage. Art and artisanship are part of the Daoist techniques of perfect behavior, ideal production, and productivity.

The *Zhuangzi* and the *Liezi* contain many stories about Daoist artists and artisans and their strange talents and abilities. Tales like that about "Cook Ding"—who is a master of carving oxen (and who therefore is more a butcher than a cook) because his knife slides "self-so" through the empty spaces in between the joints of the bones so that it does not lose any of its sharpness after nineteen years of use [38]—illustrate the Daoist art of making any kind of activity perfect by following the natural course of the Dao. Cook Ding does not act willfully or intentionally; his actions are perfectly "self-so." He follows the natural pathways and his blade occupies the empty spaces at the center of things—and therefore it is not subject to friction or loss of power and efficacy. Cook Ding and his knife imitate the workings of the Dao.

Since perfect artisanship and art follow the way of the Dao, they are methods of "bringing it on the Way." In a few instances the term *dao* can be translated not as a noun but as verb. (Chinese characters can be used as verbs, nouns, and adjectives; only the context indicates how a character is to be interpreted grammatically.) In these cases it can not only mean "to speak" or "to guide," but also "to make something happen in accord with the Dao" or to accomplish something, or, more literally, "to bring something on the Way." Cook Ding is able to bring his talents on the Way by being able to let them happen just as the Way—that is the Dao— happens. The method of the handicraft becomes the method of the Dao itself. The perfection of a profession consists in letting it take on the shape and structure of the perfect scenario. Once this is achieved, the results will be ideal and everything will be "on its Way."

Both the *Zhuangzi*[39] and the *Liezi*[40] tell the story of a Daoist master of swimming. As pointed out earlier in this book, we meet with the motif of water quite frequently in Daoist allegories and images. The Daoist symbolics of water include the idea that its movement—the seemingly "impulseless" flow downwards—is the natural movement that takes place "self-so" and *autopoietically*. Therefore it is quite plausible that the act of swimming, the going along with the natural flow of water, was a favorite image for the state of being in harmony with the Dao. This imagery was also important in the allegory of the happy fish, when Zhuangzi's strolling and the swimming of the fish was described with the same term (*you*)—which in modern Chinese still means "to swim." The art or artisanship of swimming is a paradigmatic illustration of the ability to go along with the way of the Dao.

The Daoist master of swimming described in both the *Zhuangzi* and the *Liezi* is found by Confucius who—as it is often the case in Daoist texts—approaches him for "philosophical" instructions. The story (which I will quote according to the version found in the *Liezi*) goes like this: Confucius, while traveling around with his disciples, visits a famous and dangerous waterfall. At these falls "the water dropped two hundred feet, streaming foam for thirty miles; it was a place where fish and turtles and crocodiles could not swim." These waters were too treacherous even for "natural" swimmers! Confucius, however, spots somebody who jumps down into the floods. He thinks that he saw someone committing suicide and—out of a deep Confucian feeling of sympathy and care—sends out his disciples to help the man or at least recover his body. Surprisingly, the man soon comes out of the water, strolls along the banks, and, being not at all in a depressed mood, sings a tune. Confucius is quite impressed with this sight and rushes to meet the extraordinary athlete to inquire about his most unusual methods and skills. Confucius wants to know if the swimmer has a particular "Way" (*dao*) of swimming. The strange swimmer at first denies having such a particular Way, but proceeds to give the following somewhat cryptic—at least for the non-Daoist Confucius—explanation of his art:

> No, I have no Way [*dao*]. I began with a grounding, grew up [in accordance] with the quality [of things], and completed [my] destiny. I enter the vortex with the inflow and leave with the outflow, follow the Way [*dao*] of water without acting on my own. This is how I bring it on the Way [*dao*].

Confucius does not immediately understand the swimmer's answer and asks for further clarifications. The patient master of swimming thereupon describes his way to perfection in more detail:

> I have been born on these hills and I feel comfortable on these hills. This is the grounding [of which I spoke]. I grew up with these waters

and I feel comfortable with these waters. This is [the accordance with]
the quality [of things of which I spoke]. I am so without knowing why
I am so. This is [my] destiny [of which I spoke].

This story is not only typically Daoist because of the use of water
imagery in connection with the conception of the perfect skill of
adapting to a natural course, but it is also quite typical in present-
ing the acquiring of this skill as a three-step process. Art and craftsmanship have to be cultivated and practiced. The process of
perfection is a process of increasing ability to "bring it on the Way,"
of increasing naturalness. In our story, the first step of the threefold
process of "naturing" is the "grounding," and the last step is the
fulfillment of a person's destiny—the total accordance with one's
natural place. In his educational process, the swimmer becomes
always more of a swimmer—and less of anything else. The way from
the grounding to the fulfilling of destiny is a way of integration into
a natural scenario. In the course of that process, the feelings of
"comfort," "safety," or "contentment" (the Chinese word *an* can
be translated with any of these three terms) in one's present surroundings are of utmost importance. This contentment or comfort
is the same as that which the butterfly felt when it was fluttering
around and did not know anything about Zhuang Zhou. To be
content and comfortable means to adapt perfectly to a situation
without the slightest friction and thus to be perfectly present in it.
Such a contentment and comfort allows for full authenticity in
one's present situation and is the "grounding" for being able to act
perfectly within this situation. The swimmer feels perfectly safe in
the most dangerous waters—he sings at the banks. It was his destiny to live with the water and he managed to totally adapt to this
destiny. This is what makes him a master or artist of swimming. He
has perfected his art to such a degree that he even surpasses natural
swimmers such as fish, turtles, and crocodiles.

Zhang Zhan (third century CE), an ancient Chinese commentator of the *Liezi*, explains the three steps of cultivation in the terminology of Daoist philosophy.[41] The first step, the "grounding,"
is called "simplicity"—*su*. At the beginning of cultivating an art or
a craft, one should be totally unspoiled and unshaped, just like the
uncarved wood of which the *Daodejing* speaks (chapter 37). One
has to be perfectly raw, so to speak, in order to become perfectly
polished. The second step, according to Zhang Zhan, is to practice

compliance (*shun*) or non-opposition (*bu ni*). The Chinese character for compliance is traditionally explained as depicting a leaf
floating on the water. Analogously, the Daoist apprentice has to
learn to follow the course of events without any resistance. Finally,
the completion of one's destiny, according to Zhang Zhan,
amounts to attaining full "naturalness" (*ziran*). Attaining full naturalness in turn does not allow for any theoretical reflection or representation. Once one has accomplished the perfect adapting, one
forgets any "methods." There is no knowledge about the way
when the way is performed.

The Daoist knowledge (*zhi*) without knowledge is a mastering
without mastering. The philosopher Ludwig Wittgenstein has
remarked that the "grammar" or the usage of the word "to know"
is similar to the grammar or the usage of the expressions "to be
able to," "can," and "to understand" in the sense of "to master a
technique."[42] The same is true for ancient Chinese language and
philosophy in general, and for Daoism in particular. In Daoist texts
"to know" often also means "to master." Daoist wisdom is a mastery, and this mastery consists not in actively manipulating things
or events but rather in letting things happen just "self so." The
perfect master takes him/herself back and thus enables the art
itself to come forward. As opposed to conventional (or Confucian)
learning, Daoist learning does not simply mean the "increase of
knowledge" or the "increase of skill," it rather means to gain by
loss. Chapter 48 of the *Daodejing* begins:

> Who engages in learning,
>   increases daily.
> Who hears of the Dao
>   diminishes daily.

The Daoist master of swimming cannot say that he has learnt a
particular way of swimming. He moves with the water without
doing anything. In a strict sense, he can't even swim! He has
unlearned active swimming, so that he can float with the water. He
masters the "technique" of swimming because he moves just as the
water moves. He masters the water by letting the water master
him.

Besides the kind of artists or masters who have become perfect
in performing a certain "art," like Cook Ding and the waterfall
swimmer, there are also artists or artisans who produce something.

The art of these masters creates a "thing," a piece of art, but as with the "nonproducing" masters of performance, Daoists philosophical texts often portray them while they are working. In its aesthetics Daoism does not so much focus on what is actually made or on the aesthetic object, but rather on the way of aesthetic production. More important than the product of mastery or artisanship is the "technique" of the master or artist. The following passage, which immediately follows the story of the master swimmer in the *Zhuangzi*, demonstrates this important aspect of Daoist aesthetics:

> The royal engraver Qing chipped wood to make a bellstand [for the Marquis of Lu]. When the bellstand was finished viewers were amazed, as though it were made by ghosts. When the Marquis of Lu had seen it he asked [the royal engraver]: "With which art did you make it?" The engraver answered: "I am a [simple] artisan, which art could I have? However, there is one point. When I was going to make the bellstand, I took care not to squander any of my Qi energy. I practiced the fasting of the heart to still the heart. After fasting three days, I took care not to have in my mind any thoughts about rewards and positions. After fasting five days, I took care not to have in my mind any thoughts about blame or praise, skill or clumsiness. After fasting seven days, I suddenly forgot that I had a body and four limbs. At this time my lord's court did not exist for me. While dexterity concentrated, outside distractions melted away. Then I went into the forest and observed [the trees] in regard to their natural qualities until I found the perfect stature. Then I had the complete vision of the bell stand, and I only had to put my hand on it. Otherwise, it would have all be in vain. So I could according to nature join nature. This is the reason why people wonder if [the bellstand] was made by ghosts.[43]

This story (which also shows the importance of forgetfulness) parallels the tale of the master swimmer. In place of Confucius is the Marquis of the state of Lu—Confucius's own country. The ruler asks an evidently Daoist figure, the mysterious royal engraver Qing, about his hidden powers and wonderful methods. Just like in the previous story, the Marquis is informed by the artisan that he does not really have any specific expertise, but rather a perfectly "natural" way of acting. The master engraver practices the Daoist art of meditation, the "fasting of the heart," to prepare for his work. In the course of this practice, he first forgets about the disturbing (Confucian) world around him which separates him from his "object." Then he forgets about himself, and finally he even forgets about his own art. He fasts his heart-mind—he stops thinking and deliberating—in order to perfectly adapt to the "Dao of bellstand making." Once his fasting is complete, his art unfolds by itself, as if it was performed "by ghosts." There is no visible agent that interferes in the process of art. All friction between the artist and the work of art has been dissolved. Just like the Daoist swimmer who does not resist the flow of water, the Daoist master engraver is no longer in the way of bellstand making. The engraver finally "joins nature according to nature," or, as Guo Xiang explains in his commentary, there is nothing left that separates the engraver from the course of "self-so" or *ziran*.[44]

While the story is certainly about the production of a perfect bellstand, the bellstand itself is not described. The story focuses completely on the process of production, for it is not about the bellstand as such but about "bringing bellstands on the Way." Daoist aesthetics and conceptions of art are about the production and not the characteristics of the perfect work of art. The Daoist concept of art is more a concept of artisanship than a concept of the "beautiful." And perfect artisanship is understood as the ability to perfectly follow the "natural" way of production.

Being rather an aesthetics of artisanship than an aesthetics of art, Daoist aesthetics has a distinctive concept of the "fine arts." A piece of art is not primarily understood as a depiction or "representation" of something else—as it often was in traditional Western views on art. What is more important for Daoist art and artists is how a piece of art is made and what its "effects" are. A legend about a Daoist master painter shows how a piece of art, in this case a landscape painting, is not primarily conceived of as a depiction of nature, but rather as yet another—and even more perfect—nature itself. The legend is about the miraculous skills of the painter Wu Daozi who lived in the eighth century CE and whose works are today known only in the form of later copies. It goes as follows:

> About Wu Daozi it is told that he once painted a huge landscape on the inner walls of the imperial palace. Only when he had finished the painting did he unveil it for the emperor. He pointed towards a grotto and clapped his hands. Thereupon an entrance opened and the painter entered the painting he had created and disappeared along with it right in front of the emperor's eyes.[45]

There is another quite similar legend about Wu Daozi. In order to understand this second legend one has to know that, according to ancient Chinese beliefs, rain is produced by dragons high up in the sky. The legend is that Wu Daozi once painted five dragons on the walls of the imperial palace and that every time when it rained, moisture came out of the paintings.[46]

Wu Daozi had the ability to produce perfect Daoist works of art. His paintings were not merely imitations of reality, but were themselves real. Wu Daozi's masterpiece enabled the master himself to vanish along with it. Just like the Daoist master swimmer who vanishes in the fierce waters of the waterfall and the Daoist master engraver who has to "dissolve" himself before the engraving can begin, the Daoist master painter disappears in his painting—right in the presence of the (Confucian) emperor. Wu Daozi's paintings are perfect because there is no reality gap between the "image" and its maker. The paintings are as real as the artist. Painter and painting are equally real and valid—just like in the story of the butterfly dream where both the dreamer and the dream, Zhuang Zhou and the butterfly, were equally real. The perfect painter, so to speak, resembles the perfect dreamer.

The Daoist piece of art as exemplified by the legendary paintings of Wu Daozi is not just a cunning illusion. Therefore, Daoist art did not have to be "realistic." Daoist art did not try to represent nature "realistically"—in this way it could never aspire for perfection because even the best painter is not able to paint a landscape in exactly the way it appears "out there." Daoist art does not pursue reality only to find that it can never totally reach it. A Daoist piece of art rather tries to bring reality "on the Way." The achievement of a Daoist artist consists in "giving way" to something real or natural, not to imitate it. Daoist art is not mimetic—in the sense of an ancient Greek aesthetics of representation or *mimesis*. It is rather *poietic*—or even *auto-poietic*—in that it tries to generate something real itself, not only a good depiction of something real.

According to a Chinese and Daoist understanding of art, a landscape painting is permeated by exactly the same Qi that permeates a "normal" landscape. Thus, a landscape painting and a landscape "out there" consist of basically the same "stuff" or energy. In a good painting, however, the energies of Qi can be brought into a perfect harmony. In this way, a landscape painting

can even be "better" than a landscape "out there"—or a rock gar-
den can be more "intense" than rocks "out there." Daoist landscape
paintings are real insofar as their brush strokes, the constellations of
mountains, streams, and vegetation, and even the sparse buildings
and the rare human beings who sometimes are seen in some distant valleys or on some distant banks are not merely portrayed but
indeed made or "reproduced." Therefore, an observer can actually stroll around in the scroll just as he/she can (or even better
than) in an external landscape. Not only Wu Daozi but any
observer can lose him/herself while wandering around within a
painted landscape.

Given the specific "naturalism" of Daoist art and aesthetics,
there is no primary focus on beauty. Beauty is something "ideal,"
something that is not necessarily fully present in nature. It is rather,
in traditional "Platonic" aesthetics, something transcendent or
divine. Daoist aesthetics is, on the contrary, an aesthetics of immanence. To transcend the world or reality would mean to miss it,
and Daoists aspire to be absorbed in the world and in the natural.
In the last part of this book this Daoist longing for presence, and
not for representation, will be analyzed from a more theoretical
perspective.

7. Ethics

Just as the traditional Western ideal of the "beautiful" was alien to
Daoist aesthetics, so was the traditional Western ideal of the
"good" to Daoist ethics.

Daoist "classics" such as the *Daodejing* and the *Zhuangzi* are full
of criticisms of Confucian behavior and especially of Confucian
morality. Even the legend about the Daoist master of swimming
contains a little mockery of Confucian compassion. Confucius is
emotionally disturbed by watching the Daoist swimmer and wants
to save him and to care for him—but all too no avail and certainly
not to the benefit of the swimmer. His worries are completely out
of place. At first sight, Confucius's care can be understood as an
indicator of his good character. His reaction very much resembles a
paradigmatic Confucian story found in the book of *Mencius*—a
main source for Confucian ethics. Mencius tries to prove the inherent moral goodness of humans and the inherent compassion for
others by the example of the spontaneous feeling of concern and

urge to help that anyone would feel when he/she saw a child fall into a well.[47] In the story about the Daoist swimmer, however, the spontaneous Confucian commiseration for a seemingly drowning human turns out to be highly misled—and is due to a lack of sagacity. In the story of the Daoist swimmer, Confucian empathy is not a sign of moral superiority but rather a sign of "philosophical" inferiority. In this story Confucius's morality is not wise, but ridiculous.

From a Daoist perspective, Confucian morality is a symptom of poor insight and understanding. The need for such a morality only arises when it is already too late, when one has already allowed circumstances to deteriorate to such an extent that artificial goodness is called for. Daoists try to prevent the necessity of morality in the first place. If people learn to follow the Way (*dao*) and the "own course" (*ziran*), then morality will not be required because everything will be just naturally fine. From a Daoist point of view, morality is the virtue of latecomers.

Chapter 18 of the *Daodejing* openly attacks Confucian values as being untimely, useless, and even counterproductive:

> When the great Dao is dispensed with
> then there is humanity and righteousness.
> When knowledge and smartness come out,
> then there is great falsity.
> When the six family relations are not harmonious,
> then there is filial piety and compassion.
> When state and families are in confusion,
> then there are upright ministers.

Humanity (*ren*), righteousness (*yi*), knowledge (*zhi*), and filial piety (*xiao*) are core Confucian moral values, but from a Daoist view, they are nothing but ineffective remedies in a degenerated society. And what is more, such a degenerated society is in itself the result of Confucian "falsity," of the Confucian blindness in regard to the Dao. Instead of focusing on the Dao and trying to naturally follow it in the first place, the Confucians seem to attempt to "help" the Dao once they have already failed to correspond to it. They come forth with great efforts and activities, but these only separate them further from the Way. If they would not have begun their moral engagements, the world would have been in order and harmony by itself—it is not in need of Confucian assistance. The Confucian endeavor "to make a difference" disturbs the natural order and comes too late. By introducing the distinction between good and bad, the Confucians, from a Daoist point of view, not only create goodness but also badness. Without the Confucian attempt to make the world a better place, the world would be "beyond good and evil." To prevent badness means, from a Daoist point of view, also to prevent goodness. You cannot have one without the other. Once the world is bad, the Confucian virtues will prolong its state of decay. The way to avoid social and natural sickness is not a late artificial morality but an early nonmoral prevention. In its commentary on chapter 63 of the *Daodejing*, the Legalist work *Hanfeizi* illustrates the Daoist attitude of prevention by telling the following story about the legendary doctor Bian Qiao:[48]

> Bian Qiao once had an interview with Marquis Huan of Qi. After standing for a while, Bian Qiao said: "Your highness has a disease in the capillary tubes. If not treated now, it might go deep." "I have no disease," replied Marquis Huan. After Bian Qiao went out, Marquis Huan remarked: "Physicians are fond of treating healthy people so as to display their attainments." Ten days later, Bian Qiao again had an interview and said: "The disease of Your Highness is in the flesh and skin. If not treated now, it will go still deeper." To this advice Marquis Huan made no reply. Bian Qiao went out. Marquis Huan was again displeased. After ten more days, Bian Qiao had another interview and said: "The disease of Your Highness is in the stomach and intestines. If not treated now, it will go still deeper." Again Marquis Huan made no reply to the advice. Bian Qiao went out. Marquis Huan was again displeased. After ten more days, Bian Qiao, looking at Marquis Huan, turned back and ran away. The Marquis sent men out to ask him. "Diseases that are in the capillary tubes," said Bian Qiao, "can be reached by hot water or flat irons. Those in the flesh and skin can be reached by metal or stone needles. Those in the stomach and intestines can be reached by well-boiled drugs. But after they penetrate the bones and marrow, the patients are at the mercy of the Commissioner of Life[49] wherefore nothing can be done. Now that the disease of His Highness is in his bones and marrow, thy servant has no more advice to give." In the course of five more days, Marquis Huan began to feel pain in his body, and so sent men out to look for Bian Qiao, who, however, had already gone to the Qin State. Thus ended the life of Marquis Huan. For this reason, good physicians, when treating diseases, attack them when they are still in the capillary tubes. This means that they manage things when they are small. Hence, the saintly man begins to attend to things when it is early enough.

Confucian ethics begin, so to speak, when the disease is already in the bones and marrow—and it is the Confucians' and their morality's own fault that the illness could develop that far. The Daoists, on the contrary, try to "manage things when they are small" and to "attend to things when it is early enough." They cure the body before doctors and medicaments are needed. The ancient Chinese expression for "treating the (sick) body" is *zhi shen*, the word *zhi* for "treating" is the same as the word for "ordering" in the expression "ordering the state" (*zhi guo*) and "regulating" in the expression "regulating the rivers" (*zhi shui*). Obviously, the art of curing the body was believed to be parallel to the art of governing the country and "regulating" nature. In all these cases, prevention (and thus the cultivation of a permanent awareness of symptoms that could lead to an attitude of hypochondria and fear[50]) was the Daoist key for success. A crisis has to be avoided before it begins, and the Daoists believe that the Confucians did not fully understand this and invented ethics as an inefficient remedy for their own shortcomings in cultivating the Dao.

The Daoist opposition to Confucian morality can also be understood from another perspective. If one recalls the story about Mengsun Cai, the Daoist master of mourning, one will recall the Daoist attitude towards emotions and feelings. Although Mengsun Cai wailed when the others (i.e., the Confucians in the state of Lu) were wailing, his heart was unmoved. To the Daoist sage life and death are equally valid, and thus the sage's feelings are not aroused by a simple change from one phase to the next. Because a Daoist sage practices the art of "heart fasting," he/she does not possess an "organ" for having one-sided emotions. A Daoist sage empties his/her heart and his/her ego so that emotions will take their natural course without touching him/her. A Daoist sage allows for emotions—but he/she won't be moved by them. The same is true for the moral virtues attached to certain emotions praised by Confucians (like in Mencius's example of seeing a child fall into a well). The Confucians take enormous efforts to cultivate their emotions through the practice of rites and music and to translate these emotions into social virtues (the rites are basically a pattern of virtuous behavior in society). The Daoists, on the other hand, try to eliminate emotions from the heart of the sage. The Daoist sage does not attempt to "fight" emotions and the corresponding virtues, he/she just tries to return to a pre-emotional and premoral state. The Daoist sage is shaken neither by emotions nor by virtues; he/she naturally does what is correct without any need for their guidance. The Daoist sage can be "all-right" without being good.

Emotions and morality are closely tied to each other in both Daoism and Confucianism. The Daoist view on emotions and morality corresponds to the motto of "acting out nonaction" (*wei wu wei*). When the ruler does not act, all the subjects of the state will naturally do what has to be done. When the ruler has no specific emotions (if he had specific emotions, he would be a partial leader), all emotions will be in natural harmony. And when the ruler is amoral (but, of course, not immoral), virtues will naturally unfold. These natural virtues, however, are not the false, artificial, and latecoming virtues of the Confucians. Daoist virtue is like Daoist art. It is simple and unpretentious without interest in being "good" or "beautiful."

8. Language and Thought

There are certain stereotypes that are hard to refute not because they are false but because they are half true. A common belief about Daoism is that it flatly opposes language. This belief is, for instance, expressed in Isabelle Robinet's excellent study on the history of (religious) Daoism. Robinet asserts that Daoism "has, since its origin, set at the basis of its discourse the powerlessness of the word and of thought." [51] At least in regard to Daoist *philosophy*, I do not totally agree with this statement. While philosophical Daoists certainly demand that the sage has to empty his/her heart of any thoughts and therefore also attempts to eliminate all its attachments to language, this does not mean a total negation of language and thought. [52] Just as in the political realm the nonaction (*wu wei*) of the sage ruler corresponds to the action of the subjects, so in the realm of language the silence of the sage corresponds to the speaking of the world. Silence or "linguistic fasting" is the dominating aspect of the Daoist attitude towards language, but it is by no means the only thing that it has to say. The Daoist attitude towards language parallels its widely acknowledged attitude towards action: Nonlanguage and nonaction are most important—but, in a truly Daoist paradoxical fashion, only for the sake of complete action and complete language. In a similar way, the Daoist sage's abstaining from thought is not supposed to be equated with total thoughtlessness in the world. In the following, I will discuss the Daoist philosophical attitude towards language in more detail, but what I am going to say could be equally said about the Daoist attitude towards thought (and action).

The namelessness of the Dao and the speechlessness of the ruler are important issues in the *Daodejing*. The teaching of the Dao is called the "teaching of nonspeaking" (chapters 2 and 43), the "own course" (*ziran*) of nature is said to be like "silent speech" (chapter 23), and it is said: "Who knows does not speak" (chapter 56). The name of the Dao is "unknown" (chapter 25), it "constantly has no name" (chapters 32, 37) or is simply "without name" (chapter 41). The power of the Dao and of the regent who rules in accord with it are poetically described as "nameless, uncarved wood" (chapter 37). The *Zhuangzi* too says that "the sage is nameless." [53]

The *Zhuangzi* not only asserts the namelessness of the Dao and the Daoist sage, but also explicitly discusses the parallel between namelessness and nonaction. The following passage is from its twenty-fifth chapter:

> The Dao is not selfish, therefore it has no name. It has no name, therefore it does not act. It does not act, therefore nothing is undone [*wu wei er wu bu wei*]. [54]

The Dao has no self, no individuality, no separate characteristics, no personal interests, and therefore it has no name. A specific name, title, or reputation would determine the Dao and limit it. But the Dao, just like the ruler who manifests it in human society, has no such "selfish" designation. To be without a name means to be without a specific "calling." To be without a name means to be without a specific, limited function, and therefore it also means not to act. If the Dao or the sage ruler had a name, they would have a specific position and a changeable place—they would be things among things, named by words among words.

The above quoted passage from the *Zhuangzi* appears in the context of a discussion of the perfect or "natural" social and cosmic order. It is said:

> The four seasons have their different climates. Heaven does not add [anything] to them, thus the year is completed. The five offices [in the

state government] have their different duties. The ruler does not self-ishly [take part in them], thus the state is [well] ordered. In regard to the civil and military affairs, the great man does not add [anything] to them, thus the efficacy [*de*] is thorough. The ten thousand things have their different patterns. The Dao is not selfish, therefore it has no name.

The complete year consists of the four seasons with their respective qualities—and heaven is the "empty space" that lets them take shape. Likewise, the ruler lets the activities of the state take place by allowing the five offices to do their duties. It is always the name-less and inactive that allows for the named and active to go on. That the nameless does not have a name does not mean that every-thing else either has no name or does not exist. Heaven "domi-nates" the seasons, but does not abolish them. The ruler "dominates" the officials, but does not eliminate them. The Dao "dominates" the ten thousand things, but does not annihilate them. The namelessness of the ruler does not imply that everybody in the state should be without name and title—or that there should be nobody but rulers; and the namelessness of the Dao does not imply that the ten thousand things should be nameless—or that there should be nothing else but the nameless Dao. The opposite is the case: The namelessness of the ruler and the namelessness of the Dao correspond and complete the names of the offices that organize society and the names of the ten thousand things that constitute the world. The center of the world is empty and with-out designation—but this emptiness is empty for the sake of the fullness around it. As a whole, the world consists of the *empty and the full*—and likewise the whole of language consists of the *name-less and the named*, of *silence and speech*.

   The world of the ten thousand things (or rather, following the Sinologist Christoph Harbsmeier, the world of the ten thousand *kinds* of things) is a world of forms and names. Every thing has a name and a shape. This is what constitutes a thing, and therefore the *Zhuangzi* says:

   It has a name and it has an actuality [*shi*], this is what a thing resides in.[55]

The fullness of the individual thing is made up by its name and its shape or "actuality." Names are therefore not just arbitrary designations attached to things by human willfulness, they are not just a mere convention, but rather belong to the fullness of things just like their shape or "actuality" does. A thing consists of both name and form because we can both hear about it and see it.[56] The whole cosmos, the whole process of production and reproduction, consists of those things that have a certain shape and a certain name and thus fulfill a certain function and occupy a certain time and place. Their name is part of their reality, and everything that is in reality has its specific and real name and shape. The course of things is a course of names and shapes as the following passage from the *Zhuangzi* illustrates:

> Yin and Yang respond to each other, cover each other and regulate each other. The four seasons replace each other, produce each other and extinguish each other. [. . .] Safety and danger change into each other, good luck and bad luck produce each other, slowness and swiftness convert into each other; by dispersion and concentration [things or events] take shape. All this can be accounted for by names and actualities, all this can be reflected on by subtle [thoughts].[57]

The course of nature unfolds as a course of things and events— and all these things and events can be named and have their characteristics or shapes. Because things and events take on shapes and are named, they can be reflected on—we can think about them. Language and thought can grasp their world. This is the world as it exists and as it really is, but is not what the Daoist sage focuses on. The Daoist sage affirms names, forms, and thoughts— but does not have them. He/she does not actively take part in the language and thought game of the unfolding events. If he/she would take part in this game, he/she would give up the zero-perspective. The Daoist sage stops remembering names and designations and ceases to reflect on singular things and events— to the sage everything is equally valid and nothing should be singled out by naming one thing and not the other, or by thinking one thought and not the other. Rather than this, the sage neither speaks nor thinks. So the *Zhuangzi* concludes:

> The man who has seen the Dao does neither follow where all this vanishes to nor does he/she trace the source where all this arises from. This is where the discourse ends.[58]

It is added, regarding the Dao and the Daoist sage:

> It has no name and it has no actuality. It is in the emptiness of things.[59]

The Daoist sage resides "in the emptiness of things," where there is no name and no actuality. He/she is at the center of language, silent and without a name for him/herself. At the center of the ongoing language game the Daoist sage does not debate. Those who engage in this game say that some things are true and that others are false. Others assert the opposite, and in this way the language game continues endlessly—it is an endless turning, like that of a wheel. The *Zhuangzi* criticizes non-Daoist philosophies for not taking on the zero-perspective in the language game. From a Daoist point of view other philosophies simply oppose one another, affirming one thing and thereby denying another. From the perspective of the Daoist sage these are simply complementary positions, like, for instance, the upper and lower positions of the spokes in a wheel. These "competing" philosophies fail to attain the position of the "pivot of Dao" (*dao shu*). Their disputes resemble a dispute between those who are awake and say that only being awake is real and those who are asleep and say that only being asleep is real. They are entirely dependent on their present "identifications" and do not understand that the others have their respective "identifications" and that there is no difference in reality between them. They also do not understand that in the course of change, identifications and positions will also change. The wheel of language keeps turning.

In the language game of the philosophers, one declares his/her own statements to be true and the contrasting statements to be false. The Daoist philosopher tries to get at the center of this game. The well-known second chapter of the *Zhuangzi* describes this effort—and it describes it in parallel to the Daoist philosophical effort to find a position in between life and death and in between dreaming and being awake. The butterfly allegory at the very end of this chapter summarizes the Daoist solution for each issue—the attaining of the zero-perspective—in an allegorical way. All things, shapes, and positions and opinions expressed in words have their respective place and reality. However, they do not falsify but complement one another. None of those limited perspectives expressed in "ordinary" language can claim to be more real than any other. The following passage from the second chapter of the *Zhuangzi* illustrates the Daoist "answer" to the human language game about right and wrong:

> When a human sleeps in the damp his waist hurts and he gets stiff in the joints; is that so of the loach? When he sits in a tree he shivers and shakes; is that so of the ape? Which of these three knows the right place to live? Humans eat the flesh of hay-fed and grain-fed beasts, deer eat the grass, centipedes relish snakes, owls and crows crave mice; which of the four has a proper sense of taste? Gibbons are sought by baboons as mates, elaphures like the company of deer, loaches play with fish. Mao Qiang and Lady Li were beautiful in the eyes of man; but when the fish saw them they plunged deep, when the birds saw them they flew high, when the deer saw them they broke into a run. Which of these four knows what is truly beautiful in the world?[60]

Every affirmation (*shi*) and negation (*fei*), every yes and every no, are tied to a specific perspective and position. Individual likings depend on who and what one is. Humans and animals have different tastes. All disputes in the realm of language reflect this basic pattern of diversity in the world of things and events—they reflect the distinctions (*fen*) in the world of change. Names are the manifestation of differences among things and events, and that language operates with names is a reflection of the games of change and opposition in a world of distinctions. Affirmation and negation are the basic operations in the language game, and are, from a Daoist perspective, a direct result of the distinctions among things and names. Thought is just one more reflection of this pattern. Every distinction in the world of things goes along with a distinction in names and in language, with a difference in affirming and negating. Thought translates these distinctions into mental content. The Daoist sage attempts—as the fishnet allegory illustrates—to get rid of both language and thought identifications. He/she tries to take on the zero-perspective in the world of language and thought.

In the world of distinctions everything has its position and naturally affirms this position in language and thought. For instance, the awoken Zhuang Zhou knows that he is Zhuang Zhou and, if asked, would identify himself by his name. He would deny that he is a butterfly and would not want to be called one. Language problems and debates arise when different positions and things come to confront one another. When positions or things by way of language or thought overstep their boundaries, linguistic and "ideological" conflicts will emerge. There is no remedy and no one-sided solution to these discussions—each position is real and valid for itself and so cannot accept the equal reality and validity of the other. There is no "mediation" possible, because, as another passage from the second chapter of the *Zhuangzi* explains, any mediator would either have to side with one of the positions or add another to the debate. Daoist philosophy tries to avoid both of these alternatives. It does not deny the full and equal validity of all positions—but thoroughly affirms them. The ape is right in saying that the best place to live is in a tree, and the fish is right to say that the best place to live is in the water. Viewed from the zero-perspective of the Daoist sage all positions, however contradictory they are, are equally "right."

Because they take on the zero-perspective of language, Daoist philosophers do not like discussion. They rather keep silent. But in a certain sense they are not even silent—if this is understood as taking on a position of negation that opposes all affirmations. The *Zhuangzi* states:

> Not to speak and not to be silent, this is the utmost limit of discussion.[61]

The "utmost limit" of all discussion is neither to talk nor to be silent. It is the pure emptiness of language—both positively and negatively. The silence of the sage is not just negative speech. It affirms both speech and silence, both affirmation and negation without taking part in their language and thought game. Daoist philosophy does not challenge the points of views of other philosophies; it accepts their respective "correctness" without sharing their perspectives. Daoist philosophy does not intend to silence the thought and language of others. The sage does not intend to deny the reality of the world around him/her, and an important layer of this reality is language and thought. Daoist philosophy is a philosophy that neither speaks nor argues for total silence.

Not everybody is supposed to be a Daoist sage and to take on the zero-perspective of language and thought. There cannot be a state if everybody attempts to be a ruler, and there cannot be a wheel if there is only the hub. Daoism does not proselyte—it does not intend to transform all beings into sages, to empty all "egos," and to eliminate all language and thought. The conception that every single being has to be enlightened—for instance by becoming a Buddha or by being resurrected—is alien to early Daoist philosophy. Daoist philosophy does not have a soteriology, it does not aim at individual salvation, and it is not a religion. The Daoist sage claims to be different from others, namely different from those who are different from others.

At the zero-perspective of the sage, all language and thought comes to a halt. When the second chapter in the *Zhuangzi* explains the continuous game of affirmation and negation and describes how the sage settles down at the pivot of Dao and at the center of the circle,[62] Guo Xiang comments:

> Well, affirmations and negations contradict each other and reverse each other; they follow each other without coming to an end. Therefore [the *Zhuangzi*] calls it a circle. The center of the circle is empty. For the one who regards affirmation and negation as a circle and gets at its center there is neither affirmation nor negation. And because there is neither affirmation nor negation for him/her, he/she is able to respond [*ying*] to all affirmations and negations. Because [to him/her] affirmations and negations are without limitation, his/her response is also without limitation.
>
> Nothing in the world does not affirm itself; and nothing does not negate each other. So there is one affirmation and one negation, and the two go on without limitation. Only the one who steps over into emptiness and gets to the center will be on his/her own without any baggage and have [only the Dao] as the carriage of his/her journey.[63]

In the world of language "one affirmation and one negation" connect to each other like "one yin and one yang" in the natural world[64] and constitute an endless circle. The Daoist sage gets to the language-less and thought-free center of this circle. Here, he/she accompanies the language and thought processes of the world without taking part in their contradicting but complementary movements. When the Daoist sage gets rid of all language and thought and gets what he/she wanted—which is, as the fishnet allegory pointed out, to have gotten rid of everything—then all language and thought take their own course.

Structures

1. Presence and Nonpresence—Or: The Pipe of Heaven

The images of the wheel and its variations, as well as the allegories of the butterfly dream and the fishnet, are impressive illustrations of the Dao. In this chapter I will analyze their common "architecture."

The basic structure of the image of the wheel consists of two elements—the hub and the spokes. These elements can be understood as concrete manifestations of two basic structural components of Daoist philosophy and its conceptions of humankind, the world, and the cosmos. The abstract components of many Daoist philosophical constructions are designated by two terms that are not only among the most common words in Daoist texts but in Chinese philosophy in general and even in the Chinese language of today—they are *you* and *wu*.

As a verb *you* means "being there" or "being present," and also "to have" and sometimes "to own." It can denote both the existence and the possession of something. As a noun *you* can be translated as "existence" or even as "being."

Wu is simply the negation of *you*. Accordingly it means in verbal usage "not being there" or "not being present," and also "not having" or "not possessing." As a noun it means "not-existence" or "absence;" and as the negation of "being" it is sometimes also translated as "nothing" or even "nothingness."

These terms are a pair of semantic opposites, and they are not only used in the "abstract" senses of "existence" and "nonexistence," but also sometimes more concretely in the sense of "fullness" and "emptiness." If something "is there" or if somebody "has something," there is fullness; and if nothing is there or if somebody "has nothing," then there is emptiness. In this sense *you* designates a place or spot where there is something while *wu* designates a place or spot where there is nothing. In the image of the wheel, the spokes are obviously in the space of *you*—in the space where there is something (the turning spokes cover all the space around the hub), whereas the hub is in the space of *wu*. In this image, the spokes represent the realm of fullness or existence, whereas the hub represents the realm of emptiness or nothingness. In this way the image of the wheel illustrates a core structure of Daoist philosophical "architecture." From a more formal perspective the terminological pair of *you* and *wu* can be understood as depicting the complementary opposition of *presence* and *nonpresence*, and in philosophical contexts, particularly in Daoist writings, I suggest that these words should be translated in this way.

As illustrated by the image of the wheel, the structure established by presence and nonpresence is a structure of *center* and *periphery*, of *nonchange* and *change*, and of singularity and multiplicity or of "oneness" and "twoness." The last aspect relates directly to ancient Chinese numerology. Nonpresence occupies the nonmoving center and is equated with the number one while presence circles around nonpresence and can be equated with the number two or with multiplicity. This numerological mechanism of presence and nonpresence has been described by Marcel Granet in further detail:

> The One never means anything else than the whole, while the Two is, on principle, the pair. The two is the pair which is characterized by the *alternation* (and the *communion*, but not the *sum*) of Yin and Yang. And One, the whole, is the pivot which is neither *Yin* nor *Yang*, but which the alternation of Yin and Yang relates to; it is the central square *which does not count, but which* (like the hub of which the Daoist authors say that it can make the wheel turn because it is empty) *controls the rotation* of the swastika constituted by the four rectangles into which the great quadrangle, that is, the entire space, is divided.[1]

At the center of this structure of order and efficacy is the one pivot that "is neither Yin nor Yang," that does not have any positive characteristics, and is therefore totally "empty." Ancient

Chinese numerology identified the empty pivot with the number one—and not with the number zero!—because the pivot has to be singular. However, this One "does not count," as Marcel Granet explains, because it is empty and nonpresent. The empty nonpresent oneness, as he further notes "never means anything else than the whole." The singular hub is identified with the entire wheel, and the empty center of any perfect scenario can be identified with its entirety. The alternation of Yin and Yang, the two rubrics with which all the ten thousand things can be classified, circulates around the singular pivot.[2] The structure of the perfect scenario consists of a nonpresent, singular center and a present periphery based on multiplicity. This structure is, and Marcel Granet points this out as well, the basic structure of the ancient Chinese conception of space. The ancient Chinese believed that the earth was a square (surrounded by the "four seas"). The space of the earth is further divided into a central square enclosed by four rectangles that create the shape of a swastika. The rectangles are supposed to move around the center. Obviously, this structure, although square, parallels that of the wheel:

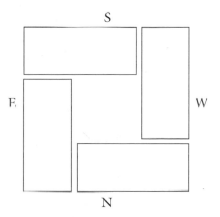

FIGURE 4
The ancient Chinese conception of space, following
Marcel Granet.[3]

The composite structure of presence and nonpresence is connected to the conceptions of space. The "abstract" order of presence and nonpresence is also directly related to the symbolics of numbers. Nonpresence corresponds to singularity, wholeness, and the number one, while presence corresponds to twoness and the multiplicity that associates and results from it. In their structural integration these opposites form the pattern of a perfect scenario. Marcel Granet continues his above quoted discussion of ancient Chinese conceptions of space with some more detailed remarks on numerology—without mentioning a very important and well-known chapter of the *Daodejing*:

> The One is the indivisible which cannot be added to, because it is not a synthesis of odd and even numbers; it is the unity which cannot have any other value than 1 since it is the all-inclusive whole. It also cannot be separated from the Two because in it all opposing contrasts which are still united—left and right, top and bottom, front and back, circle and square, the assembly of Yang and the assembly of Yin—are absorbed. Expressed in numbers the whole, insofar as it integrates unity and the pair, is contained in all odd numbers and, above all, in the number Three (which is One plus Two). [. . .] Thus, the series of numbers begins with the 3.[4]

The central unity is alone and therefore all-one at the same time, it is wholeness and singularity, it is unity and totality. The number one symbolizes this all-oneness. It "absorbs" all twoness. Just as the hub unites left and right and top and bottom, the one is the pivot of two, uniting and integrating the manifold. Oneness and twoness, presence and nonpresence, center and periphery constitute the "world." The number that symbolizes the combination of oneness and twoness is—and this can be calculated without great mathematical skill—the number three. Therefore, only with three can multiplicity and the number series begin. One and two, nonpresence and presence, are the structural elements of multiplicity, but multiplicity itself only begins when these two elements are combined. This is why it begins with the number three. With "threeness" the diversity and variety of the world and the cosmos begins to unfold.

The well-known first lines of the forty-second chapter of the *Daodejing* are nothing else but a formulaic description of this numerical structure of the cosmos:

> The Dao generates Oneness.
> Oneness generates Twoness.
> Twoness generates Threeness.
> Threeness generates the ten thousand things.

In connection with the numerological analysis of Marcel Granet quoted above, these somewhat cryptic lines can be quite easily interpreted: The Dao as the structure of the perfect scenario is firstly symbolized by the One and by oneness. The Dao is at the same time emptiness and wholeness, it integrates these two aspects into the One. Being wholeness, the oneness of the Dao entails twoness—the twoness of Yin and Yang, top and bottom, and so forth. Thus it is the combination of oneness and twoness which "generates" everything that is present, which generates the "ten thousand things." Oneness and twoness generate threeness, and threeness is the fountain head of multiplicity, of the manifold world of the ten thousand.

Numerological symbolics of oneness, twoness, and threeness were not only developed in ancient China, but also in ancient Europe and in many other civilizations. In China an important traditional interpretation associated oneness with the Dao, twoness with Yin and Yang or heaven and earth, and threeness with heaven, earth, and man, but there have also been other concretizations of that basic numerology. The first lines of the forty-second chapter of the *Daodejing* represent a kind of numerological structure of Daoist and ancient Chinese philosophy and cosmology. This "abstract" deep structure can be applied in various philosophical and nonphilosophical theoretical constructs.

In the Mawangdui silk manuscripts of the *Daodejing*, the above quoted beginning of chapter 42 immediately follows the last lines of chapter 40 in the standard edition of the text. (The Guodian bamboo manuscripts contain a version of the fortieth chapter but none of the forty-second.) These last lines read:

> The things of the world are generated from presence [*you*].
> Presence is generated from nonpresence [*wu*].

These two sentences are not only "physically," but also stylistically and semantically connected to the beginning of chapter 42. While this chapter discusses the "generation" of oneness, twoness, and threeness, chapter 40 discusses the generation of presence and nonpresence—or *you* and *wu*. It is obvious that Daoism connected numerology with these basic cosmological or structural aspects.

The Dao is identified with the number one and with oneness in its double sense, and also with emptiness and nonpresence. Wang

Bi, the eminent commentator of the *Daodejing*, remarks in regard to chapter 42: "Oneness can be called nonpresence [*wu*]." The Dao, oneness, and nonpresence are associated with each other. The sentence "The Dao generates Oneness" is therefore semantically analogous to saying that the Dao generates nonpresence. Accordingly, the sentence "Oneness generates Twoness" from chapter 42 is equivalent to the sentence "Presence is generated from nonpresence [*wu*]," because twoness symbolizes presence just as oneness symbolizes nonpresence. If oneness generates twoness, then this also means that nonpresence generates presence, or in more concrete terms, that emptiness generates fullness or that the center generates the periphery.

Finally, following the same pattern of correspondence, the sentences "Twoness generates Threeness. Threeness generates the ten thousand things" from chapter 42 are analogous to the sentence "The things of the world are generated from presence" from chapter 40. The threeness mentioned in chapter 42 is the beginning of the series of numbers (as Marcel Granet pointed out) and therefore the symbol for the multiplicity in the realm of the ten thousand things that are mentioned in chapter 40. Just as twoness generates threeness and therefore also the ten thousand things, so presence generates the "things of the world."

The beginning of chapter 42 and the end of chapter 40 are in perfect correspondence. In addition, both passages are constructed on the basis of the same pattern as the image of the wheel from chapter 11. Chapter 42 expresses this structure with numerical symbols, while chapter 40 expresses it with the concepts of nonpresence and presence.

It remains to be asked in which specific way oneness and twoness, emptiness and fullness, nonpresence and presence, can "generate" the world and its multiplicity. Are they the ultimate origin of Being or the creative force behind all things in the cosmos? As explained earlier in this study, early Daoist philosophy (that is, previous to Wang Bi) does not seem to have conceived of the Dao, oneness, nonpresence, or emptiness as a first creator or mover. Many early texts explicitly state that the structure of nonpresence and presence is not a structure of "creation" in the sense of a genealogy or a Judaeo-Christian *creatio*. Specifically the *Zhuangzi*, and Guo Xiang's commentary, demonstrate why the Daoist connection between nonpresence, presence, and the multiplicity of things (or between oneness, twoness, and threeness) does *not* necessarily have to be interpreted as a connection of "historical" origination or causation.

A beautiful passage in the *Zhuangzi* illustrates poetically that the interplay between presence and nonpresence or emptiness and fullness—which can well be understood as the basis of all things in the world—is not a diachronic chain of causation or origination, but is rather a pattern of synchronicity and "co-evolution." All structural elements are supposed to cooperate synchronically so that the world will be productive and effective—and if they don't, the world will be in disorder. The second chapter of the *Zhuangzi* introduces a Daoist master named Ziqi who successfully lost his "I." A student approaches him and inquires how he had done this. The master answers with an image. He tells the student about three kinds of pipe music. First, there is the flute music of men who blow through bamboo pipes. Then there is the pipe music of the earth. This is made by the wind when it blows through all kinds of holes and hollows. The description of the "pipe of the earth" is one of the poetic gems of the *Zhuangzi*:

> That hugest of clumps of soil blows out breath, by name the "wind."
> It is not now starting up, but whenever it does ten thousand hollow
> places burst out howling, and don't tell me you have never heard how
> the hubbub swells! The recesses in mountain forests, the hollows that
> pit great trees a hundred spans round, are like nostrils, like mouths,
> like ears, like sockets, like bowls, like mortars, like pools, like puddles.
> Hooting, hissing, sniffing, sucking, mumbling, moaning, whistling,
> wailing, the winds ahead sing out AAAH!, the winds behind answer
> EEEH!, breezes strike up a tiny chorus, the whirlwind a mighty chorus. When the gale has passed, all the hollows empty, and don't tell
> me you have never seen how the quivering slows and settles![5]

Given this exquisite description, the student obviously understands what the master means by speaking of the pipe music of the earth. However, he still does not understand how the pipe of heaven sounds and asks for further clarification. The master answers only by posing a rhetorical question:

> Well, [the pipe of heaven] blows in ten thousand variations and lets
> [the ten thousand things sound] by themselves. When all things take
> [their sounds] from themselves, who should stir them up?[6]

The master ends with a pun. Like the fishnet allegory and many modern-day jokes the last of three seemingly parallel parts is unlike the first two. The pipe of men is blown by men. The pipe of the earth is blown by the wind—but who blows the pipe of heaven? The answer is: No one—everything in the world "ultimately" makes its own sound. There is no great blower behind this great concert of sounds. Seen as a whole, the world is complete in itself and has no "creator" beyond it. It is just like chapter 25 of the *Daodejing*, which states (see above): Given the context of the Dao, everything follows its "own course." The great scenario has no external "blower"—it allows for all things to sound, live, or move "naturally" by themselves. The greatest, all encompassing pipe—the cosmos—sounds itself, there is no cause and no origin. The pipe of men and the pipe of the earth needs some initial puff, but the pipe of heaven doesn't.

But why does the great cosmic pipe need no one to blow it, how does it blow simply by itself? The answer lies in the chosen image. A pipe is just another illustration of the basic structure of the perfect Daoist scenario: it is emptiness surrounded by fullness, nonpresence integrated with the presence around it. The great Dao functions like a wheel, a bellows, or a valley—to name some other images from the *Daodejing*. It is an *autopoietical* or self-generating pattern of *wu* and *you*.

That the Daoist structure of emptiness and fullness, of center and periphery, of singularity and multiplicity, of nonpresence and presence, is exactly *not* a structure of causation, origination, and creation but rather one of self-generation is made clear by Guo Xiang's commentary on the allegory of the pipe of heaven:

> This is the pipe of heaven. Well, regarding the pipe of heaven, how should there be yet another thing? When things such as those hollows [of the earth] and holes in the bamboo [flutes of men] come together with all things that exist, then in their unity they form the one heaven. Nonpresence is nothing but nonpresence; and therefore it cannot bring presence into existence. When the present does not yet exist, it cannot produce existence. Given this, who should then bring existence into existence? [What exists] exists as one piece through itself.[7]

Heaven, Guo Xiang further explains, is in this context not the designation for that blue stretch of sky above our heads. Here it is rather the name that denotes all the "ten thousand things" in their entirety. Outside of this closed totality there is no creator or origin. Everything that exists, in its entirety, exists by itself, and at the center of this entirety of presence is "nothing"—or more precisely, nonpresence (*wu*). This is the "Dao of heaven" (*tian dao*). In its entirety the pattern of nonpresence and presence exists "as one piece." If the nonpresent center is to be understood as an "origin," it has to be understood as a purely immanent origin. This origin does not exist before or external to what it originates. Guo Xiang points out in his commentary on another passage in the *Zhuangzi* that neither the Dao, nonpresence (*wu*), the "self-so," or the "own course" (*ziran*) can exist prior to (*xian*) things.[8] The Dao and the world of things naturally coexist.

Unlike, for instance, Christianity, Daoist philosophy does not generally believe in a creator who precedes the world. The Dao does not precede or create the structure of *wu* and *you*, it rather *is* this structure. The Dao of heaven is the pipelike, dynamical pattern of nonpresence and presence.

2. Daoist Signs—Or:
The Difference between Dao and God

In its most "abstract" dimension, the Dao is a perfect pattern of order that is constituted by *wu* and *you*, by nonpresence and presence. This basic structure of early Daoist philosophy corresponds to specific concepts of significance —and of the most significant. In this chapter, I will try to explore the "architecture of meaning" in ancient Chinese Daoism and how it compares to similar structures in the Western tradition. What I find of particular interest is how a structure of meaning is reflected in the conceptions of the most meaningful being of all, which, in the case of the Western tradition, was often called "God." Thus I will first compare ancient Daoist concepts of signs and meaning to Western ones, and then try to show how these different understandings of meaning and signification have influenced different understandings of the "highest" being.

Modern and postmodern Western philosophers (like, for instance, Michel Foucault and Richard Rorty) have described traditional Western concepts of meaning and signification as largely "representational." This term refers to a quite simple relation between signs and what they mean or signify, or more technically, between the signifier and the signified. More often than not, the relation between the signifier and the signified is understood as one of representation. The signifier is supposed to somehow *represent* the signified. A classical expression of this relation is presented in Aristotle's short treatise *De Interpretatione*:

> Now spoken sounds are symbols of affections in the soul, and written marks symbols of spoken sounds. And just as written marks are not the same for all men, neither are spoken sounds. But what these are in the first place signs of—affections of the soul—are the same for all; and what these affections are likenesses of—actual things—are also the same.[9]

Following Aristotle's analysis, the actual things in the world somehow provide the human soul with accurate perceptions—the soul forms mental "likenesses" of the things in the world. These likenesses are further "translated" into spoken sounds by human beings. We give certain names to the things perceived by the soul, and these names differ from language to language. Finally the spoken words are once more "translated" into written symbols, into writing. Again, these written symbols differ from script to script, from alphabet to alphabet.

The world of "symbols" begins, according to Aristotle's account, with language. As long as things only affect the soul, these affections are the same for everyone. Everyone is supposed to have the same "likeness" of the same worldly thing in his or her soul. But when it comes to symbols that "represent" the things and their likenesses, differences arise. What we call these things and their likenesses depends entirely on language. The likenesses in the soul are not "symbols" according to Aristotle—they do not symbolize but rather transpose things. We cannot arbitrarily determine a "sign" for "representing" things in our soul, but we have to decide arbitrarily what to call these things once we start to speak about them. There is a substantial difference between the things and their likenesses in our soul, on the one hand, and between written and spoken symbols on the other: By affecting our soul, the thing is mentally *present* in our soul. But in language, we have to *re-present* the thing and its "likeness." In language, the true presence of the thing is lost and comprehended only through "artificial" representation, through "symbols."

There is a gap between the presence of things and the symbols of sound and script that represent them. This gap of representation constitutes the "sign" and its "meaning." There are two "worlds" now—one of representing signs, and one of actual things and thoughts that are "meant" or "signified" by these signs. Things and "likenesses" are actual and truly real; they are, as Aristotle points out, "the same for all men." Symbols are not the same for all men and are therefore somewhat less real, they are "only" symbols of the really real and the true. Signs and representations constitute a second level of reality, they produce a split in the world: things and thoughts are present, and they can be represented by symbols.

The idea that a signifier relates to a truly present thing has been very influential for traditional Western conceptions of the artistic image. A legend from ancient Greece illustrates how paintings were conceived of as illusive representations of present things. Pliny records a painting competition between the two Greek artists Zeuxis and Parrhasios. The story states that Zeuxis first displayed a picture of grapes that was so realistic that birds came to eat them. Then Parrhasios brought a painting covered with a sheet. Zeuxis, still proud of his success, urged Parrhasios to quickly remove this sheet, but then realized that the sheet itself was the painting! He admitted his defeat because while he had only been able to deceive birds, Parrhasios had been able to deceive him. This story obviously connects with the ancient Greek ideal of art as perfect resemblance—which was strongly criticized by Plato in his *Republic*. The basic principle of this type of painting was the representation of nature.[10]

A second story recorded by Pliny further exemplifies this ideal. The story is also about Zeuxis and a painting of grapes. This time, he had painted a boy carrying some grapes, and again birds came to feed. Zeuxis then got a little angry with himself and said: "I have painted the grapes better than the boy. If I had painted the boy as perfectly, the birds would have been afraid."[11]

Both legends operate with a pattern of the sign in which the signifier (the paintings) and the signified (the grapes, the sheet, and the boy) have to be as similar as possible, but still be discernible in nature. In order for the competition to make sense, both paintings have to be "unmasked" as mere paintings or signs. The painting has to be as *realistic* as possible to be a *good* painting—but, of course, it has to be *unreal* in order to be a good *painting*. The signifiers have to appear to be like the signified, but they also have to be essentially different from them. The signifiers have to represent the signified as closely as possible, but they are not supposed to truly present the signified. The representations are merely "copies" of an "original," and this difference has to be detected for them to be accepted as paintings. Zeuxis has to find out that Parrhasios's sheet is not a sheet, but a representation, in order to acknowledge his superior skill. The core of the competition is *deception*. Art is the more perfect the more deceptive it is. Its representation is more stunning the closer it resembles *and* differs from the real. At the heart of representation is the ambivalence of apparent reality and actual deception.

The pattern of representation is based on the gap between the full reality of the signified and the deceptive reality of the signifier. Within this pattern the two constituting elements (signifier and signified) are not equally real. One *is* more than the other. This representational structure creates an "ontological" hierarchy between the signifier and the signified.

The "ontological difference" entailed in this pattern is quite alien to the ancient Daoist philosophy of presence. Daoist philosophers did not tend to ascribe different levels of reality, validity, or authenticity to the signifier and the signified. Regarding names (as signifiers) and actualities (as signified) as the components of the thing, the *Zhuangzi* says:

> It has a name and it has an actuality [*shi*], this is what a thing resides in.[12]

A thing consists of a name and an actuality. The name of a thing is not thought of as an arbitrary linguistic addition to its actuality, but rather as an equally real part of it. The name "horse" and the actual horse together constitute the "thing" horse. Signifier and signified are both present with the presence of the thing. The name is not a secondary "representation" of the thing, but rather believed to be an inherent aspect of its presence.

The semiotic pattern of an equal presence of the signifier and the signified also underlies the above mentioned legends about the Daoist painter Wu Daozi.[13] Wu Daozi's paintings excelled by being as real as what they presented. The painted grotto was as real as any real grotto, and this was also true of the painted dragons. These paintings were believed to be perfect not through perfect deception but through perfect realization.

The difference between a semiotics of presence and a semiotics of representation can be depicted as such:

	present	re-presenting
Pattern of Presence	signified — signifier	
Pattern of Representation	signified—	—signifier

From a traditional Western point of view, the Daoist semiotic pattern of presence is somewhat odd because it ascribes full presence to the signifier. On the basis of the above quoted Aristotelian conception of the sign, the sign only comes into being when the presence of the thing that is either in the world or the soul is somehow transcended in language. This framework more or less defines the symbol as a symbol of representation and thus does not allow for symbolics on the level of pure presence—the soul is *not* supposed to perceive the thing in the form of a mental "symbol," it is supposed to contain its present "likeness." A semiotic pattern of presence, on the other hand, does not suppose any "ontological" split in the world that would separate a mere "symbolical" realm of representation (such as, for instance, language) from a truly present realm of things or ideas.[14]

It may be said that as the Daoists did not intend to devaluate the world of the dreamer, they also did not intend to devaluate the name or the work of art. Their semiotics of presence could accept everything as equally real and "worldly," regardless of its nature. They did not see why a name or an image was less genuine than anything else.

The difference between a semiotics of presence and that of representation can be identified as a structural reason for many differences between Daoist and Western philosophies. The philosophy of language and aesthetics—as discussed above—are good examples of such differences. Another, more specific example is the issue of memory, which is of particular importance for understanding

the Butterfly Dream allegory in a Daoist way. In connection with
a pattern of representation, memory can be conceived of primarily
as re-membrance in Western philosophies, while Daoist and other
Chinese philosophies conceived of it rather as an unbroken con-
tinuation of presence.[15] Even such important conceptions as the
idea of a "highest being" can be distinguished on the basis of different paradigms of presence and representation. Both in the
Western Christian tradition and in Daoism the most important
"entities"—God and the Dao—were described as the ineffable—
but on the basis of different paradigms of the sign, the ineffable
could have very different meanings.

It has been frequently mentioned that the Dao is without a
name. Being without a name, the Dao is surely not adequately
described in language; it is some kind of an ineffable ultimate.
Christian theology, especially so-called negative theology, also
pointed out the ineffability of God. If, however, Daoist and
Christian philosophy were operating with different concepts of
the sign, then it is likely that this ineffability has a specific significance in each tradition. Conceptions of the unnamed have
something to do with conceptions of the named, and if conceptions of the named differ, then conceptions of the unnamed may
also differ. Or, in other words: while the *ineffable within a paradigm of representation tends to be that which cannot be represented, the ineffable within a paradigm of presence tends to be that
which is nonpresent.*

A famous philosopher of the ineffable in the Western theological tradition is the so-called Pseudo-Dionysius or Dionysius the
Areopagite, an author of the fifth or sixth century CE whose real
name is unknown. Pseudo-Dionysius repeats and varies the following thought: God alone is utmost and singular presence; he is
the One, and the world is merely his own representation. On the
one hand, there is nothing in the world "lacking a share in that
One which in its utterly comprehensive unity uniquely contains all
and every thing beforehand"[16]; everything that exists shares in the
unity of that One. On the other hand, however, God or the One
is never fully present in the world that represents him as his own
sign. God is the utmost reality and presence, and the world of
men, of human action and human words, is a sign and a representation of his reality. However, God's representation of the world of
men can never be as fully real and present as He himself is—just

like the grapes and the sheet in the paintings of Zeuxis and Parrhasios could never be quite as real as real grapes or sheets. The representation is a true *image* of the present from which it originates—but being an image it *is* not as true. Thus, even if everything in the world is a sign of God and documents God's reality, God himself is still always essentially beyond that which only represents him. The Pseudo-Dionysius says: "But no unity or trinity, no number or oneness, no fruitfulness, indeed, nothing that is or is known can proclaim that hiddenness beyond every mind and reason of the transcendent Godhead which transcends every being. There is no name for it nor expression." [17]

The world continuously indicates God and God alone, but these indications themselves are never fully adequate. They are always a sign of God and by being a sign, they are not the real thing. God's relation to the human world resembles, as a core image of Pseudo-Dionysius explains, the relation *between a seal and its impressions*.[18] The impression is always similar to the seal—it is its genuine sign—but it is also always dissimilar to it—it is never the seal itself. Pseudo-Dionysius further comments on this difference by saying:

> [. . .] scripture itself asserts that God is dissimilar and that he is not to be compared with anything, that he is different from everything and, stranger yet, that there is none at all like him. Nevertheless words of this sort do not contradict the similarity of things to him, for the very same things are both similar and dissimilar to God. They are similar to him to the extent that they share what cannot be shared. They are dissimilar to him in that as effects they fall so very far short of their Cause and are infinitely and incomparably subordinate to him.[19]

Pseudo-Dionysius describes the deficiency of the representation in comparison to presence in quite drastic terms. The semiotics of negative theology do not merely discuss the relation between signifiers and the signified, but the relation between God and the world. Here, literally everything is understood on the basis of the structure of presence/representation; and the present is praised as ultimately more real and perfect than its representation.

Pseudo-Dionysius's theology is an extreme type of Western "representationalism." The realm of representation is portrayed as "infinitely and incomparably subordinate" to the realm of presence. A representation can never be as real as the present, and by being "similar" it is also "dissimilar." By definition, that which is similar also has to be dissimilar because if it were not, it would not be only similar, but identical. The pattern of presence and representation necessarily introduces a gap of authenticity between its two constitutive components.

The "infinite and incomparable" deficiency of the representation in regard to the present creates a paradox of great theological relevance: That which is most important to name turns out to be unnamable. The more one tries to represent the present, the more the ultimate difference between the two realms of representation and presence becomes obvious. At the same time, the flaw of representation only confirms the immaculateness of the presence. The more evident it becomes that representation is flawed, the more obvious it is that the present is immaculate. The pattern of presence and representation fits the pattern of negative theology: If God is the immaculate as such, he must be the utmost presence and be ultimately nonrepresentable. If he could be perfectly represented, he would no longer be himself. By becoming similar to himself, he would also become dissimilar from himself.

The semiotics of representation tends to deify presence—at least in the case of negative theology. With Pseudo-Dionysius, presence becomes a transcendent beyond and God becomes the absolute signified, represented by all things in the world as His signifiers—and thus presented by none.

Negative theology and Pseudo-Dionysius use the image of the seal and its impressions to illustrate the relation between God and the world, between the ineffable and its names. This image is also an image of a semiotics of representation. A Daoist semiotics of presence can be illustrated with another image—namely that of the wheel.

In the image of the wheel, the unnamed, the Dao, corresponds to the hub, while the realm of names and forms corresponds to the space of the spokes. Unlike the relation between the seal and its impressions, the relation between the hub and the spokes is not one of presence and representation, but rather a relation between nonpresence and presence. The empty hub is nonpresent, but it nevertheless balances and unites the spokes that present the wheel.

There is an "ontological" hierarchy included in the relation between the seal and its impressions: by representing the seal, the impressions are of less "being" or reality—they are always secondary. Between the hub and the spokes there is not such a hierarchy. The spokes in no way "represent" it—and they do not lack any authenticity of being in comparison with the hub. Ancient Chinese philosophy in general, and Daoist thought in particular, does not tend to suppose an "ontological" gap between the realms of representation and presence. An ancient Chinese "semiotics of presence" rather conceives of *both* the signifier and the signified as equally present. The realm of the present includes everything that "is" (*you*); and between this realm of presence (the space of the spokes) and the realm of nonpresence (the space of the hub) there is no "representational" relation. As opposed to the "representationalism" of the Pseudo-Dionysius, the ineffable is not equated with the absolute present. The Daoist ineffable, the Dao, is rather the nonpresent pivot around which everything that is present revolves. It is that central element in the world that is empty of both name and form. As opposed to a semiotics of representation, the Daoist semiotics of presence can be explained on the basis of the following pattern:

nonpresent (and ineffable)	present
Dao	signified — signifier

The Dao is *not* ineffable because it is beyond any adequate representation, but rather because it simply does not belong to the realm of the interplay between names and forms. The Dao, like God, is ineffable; but its ineffability is of a very different sort. The specific ineffability of the Dao is discussed in a short essay entitles "On the Nameless" (*Wu ming lun*) attributed to the Neo-Daoist philosopher He Yan (third century CE). This text relies on both earlier Daoist and Confucian ideas. In particular, He Yan discusses the philosophical paradox that the nameless, once it is called the "nameless," is no longer nameless. He tries to show that even though the nameless—the Dao and the *famous* sage rulers who manifests it—is called the nameless it is still different from everything "normally" named:

Being pointed out by people brings about that which has a name. Not being pointed out is that which has no name. When the sage is named the nameless and pointed out as the one not pointed out, and when the Dao is taken to be the nameless, and the not pointed out to be the great,[20] then the nameless may be spoken of as having a name and the not pointed out may be spoken of as pointed out. But does this mean to be of the same function as that which is pointed out and named?

This is to be explained on the basis of having the nonpresent [*wu*] and therefore also having all which is present [*you*]. At the center of all that which is present there is the companion of the nonpresent, and this is not the same as that which is present.

No matter how far apart things are, things of the same kind will respond to each other; and no matter how near they are, things of different kinds contradict each other. It is like the Yang in the Yin and the Yin in the Yang. Each attracts and responds to its own kind. The summer is Yang, but its nights, though distant from the winter, are nevertheless Yin like the winter. The winter is Yin, but its days, though distant from the summer, are nevertheless Yang like the summer. Thus the summer nights and the winter days are different from the near and like the far. Only when such likeness and difference are fully comprehended can the discourse on the nameless be understood. How does it happen to be this way?

Well, the Dao alone is nonpresence. With the beginning of heaven and earth there is all that which is present.[21] Now, what about that which is called the Dao? Because it can still have the function of nonpresence, it is not-there, even if it dwells in the land of that which has names. It has the contour of the nameless. It is as being in the distant body of Yang while forgetting that it is itself of the kind of the distant Yin.

Xiahou Xuan[22] said: "Heaven and earth move along their 'own course' (*ziran*). The sage functions along with his/her 'own course' (*ziran*)." The "own course" is the Dao. The Dao is originally without name. Thus Laozi said: "[. . .] forced to give it a name [. . .]"[23] Confucius praised sage-emperor Yao, as being "so great that he could be given no name" and continued to say, "How majestic was his accomplishment!"[24] It is clear that to give a name perforce is merely to give an appellation on the basis of common understanding. If the sage emperor Yao would have really had a name, how could [Confucius] have said that "he could be given no name?" Only because he was nameless could he have been named with all names of the world—but are these really his names?

If from this illustration one still does not understand, it would be like looking at the eminence of Mount Tai and yet saying that matter is not extensive.[25]

He Yan identifies the nameless with the sage emperor, the Dao, and with nonpresence. Nameless nonpresence is not lost with the "beginning of heaven and earth." It is the "origin" of presence in the midst of presence. Even while "dwelling in the land of presence" it "is not-there." One may say: it dwells not-there in the midst of what is there like the hub lies in the midst of the wheel. He Yan uses another example: summer nights and winter days. Nights belong to the rubric of the dark and the cold, they are Yin, but in summer, the season of Yang, they are there in the midst of a segment of brightness and warmth. Vice versa, days belong to the rubric of the bright and the warm, they are Yang, but in winter, the season of Yin, they are in the midst of a segment of darkness and cold. Nonpresence resembles a summer night: being itself dark and cold it nevertheless is at the center of a sequence of brightness and warmth.

Even though the nameless is an integral part of the named, it can still be perfectly nameless. Names can be attributed to it from the perspective of that which has names, but it does not thereby lose its namelessness. Its names, like the "nameless," the "great," or the "Dao," are nothing but pseudonyms. The *Zhuangzi* states:

> The Dao cannot be present; and that which is present cannot be nonpresent. If it is called by the name of Dao then this is to give it a pseudonym.[26]

The namelessness of the Dao is not really obscure. It is not the negative namelessness of the seal that disappears when its signs are seen. Given the pattern of representation, God and the present are nameless because they necessarily retreat when there are signs and names. In the Daoist semiotics of presence, names and the nameless, presence and nonpresence, *coexist*. A seal always precedes the impression, but a hub always coexists with the spokes. The Daoist nameless nonpresence is not transcendent, it is immanent in the presence of the named.

The Dao is not "beyond" names, it is simply the unnamed element in the midst of all names. It is not that names "fail" to fully describe the Dao, it is rather that the Dao cannot be given a name because it has no qualities. The perfection of God does not allow him to be adequately represented with necessarily limited and incomplete names—God is too *full* to be named. The

Dao, however, is too *empty* to be named. God is ineffable because He is not "representable," whereas the Dao is ineffable because it is nonpresent.

A semiotics of representation is based on the distinction between a realm of representation and a realm of presence—and this distinction goes along with the distinction between the signifier and the signified. A semiotics of presence is based on a different distinction. Here the main distinction is between nonpresence and presence, and both signifier and the signified "dwell" in the realm of presence.[27]

In the negative theology of Pseudo-Dionysius the world, as a similar-dissimilar impression, continuously indicates a present, but transcendent, God. The world is therefore always somewhat deficient and "lags behind." In the Daoist semiotics of presence, the Dao is not "indicated" by the things of the world, and so these things do not fall short of it. There is no "structural" deficiency of the world in regard to the Dao. Consequently, Daoism did not develop a semantics of misery to characterize the world of the named. Daoism does not see the world of men as necessarily lacking God's perfection, and so has no notion of "original sin." A Christian semiotics of representation can easily be translated into a semantics of human insufficiency. In Daoism, man was not made in the image of God, and therefore was never conceived of as ultimately betraying His own creation. A Christian semiotics of representation introduced a split between God and God's image. The Daoist semiotics of presence never introduced such a split between the Dao and the world of things and man. Thus there was also never a need for a reconciliation, or resurrection—or for grace. This may be a reason why Daoism, to put it in Nietzschean terms, found it much easier than Christianity to say yes to the genuineness of life without any *ressentiment*.

Perspectives

1. Daoism and Chan (or: Zen) Buddhism

Daoism and Chan Buddhism (or "Zen Buddhism" as it is called in its Japanese form) are closely related. When Buddhism established itself as one of China's main religions in the fourth and fifth century CE, it also began to profoundly influence the history of Chinese philosophy. From this time on, Buddhism and Daoism were often seen as having somewhat similar worldviews, and the early translators of Buddhist texts often fell back on Daoist terminology when they tried to find suitable Chinese words for "alien" Buddhist concepts. The modern Chinese philosopher Feng Youlan (1895–1990) accurately summed up the Buddhist "reinforcement" of Daoism by saying: "The combination of Daoism and Buddhism resulted in Chanism, which I should like to call a philosophy of silence."[1]

The creation of Chan Buddhism was an immediate effect of the "Sinization" or "Daoization" of Buddhism. The Chan Buddhists of the Tang Dynasty (618–906 CE) were often as familiar with ancient Daoist classics as they were with Buddhist sutras, and their teachings are indeed an amalgamation of both traditions. The many parallels between Daoism and Chan, however, sometimes lead interpreters to understand Daoism as being merely an earlier variety of Chan, so that the old Daoist philosophers appear as early Buddhists. If one agrees, as I do, with Feng Youlan's observation that Chan Buddhism is the result of the *combination* of Daoism and Buddhism, then one has to acknowledge not only the parallels, but also the differences between

Daoism and Chan. In the following, I will briefly outline some of the differences that are often less noted than the many similarities.

Daoist philosophy takes the body very seriously.[2] Although Buddhism, especially in its early Indian forms, also cares about the body and even includes yogic practices, it focuses much more on the mind and its "spirituality." In China for instance, Indian Yogacara Buddhism developed into a school called the "Consciousness-Only-Teaching"—a form of Chinese Buddhism that is slightly older than Chan. The "Consciousness-Only" school introduced an extremely complex theory of an eightfold structured mind and gave rise to a kind of Buddhist idealism that viewed the world as a construct of consciousness activity. Chan Buddhism did not follow such a "totalization" of mind, and its "negative method" (to follow Feng Youlan) of philosophy and meditation aimed at attaining enlightenment by eliminating any specific theories of the mind (and even any specific theories of the Buddha and of Buddhahood). Still, such criticisms of consciousness could not avoid a relation to Buddhist notions of the mind. This is to say that while Chan Buddhism had a somewhat "negative" attitude towards these problems, it was nevertheless very much concerned with them, and so was, in a certain sense, still a "philosophy of mind."

Early Daoism did not react to a Buddhist philosophical background, and it did not develop into a philosophical discourse in which consciousness was a central issue. The most important ancient Chinese word for the "mind" was *xin*—which literally meant the *heart*. The heart was believed to be the seat of the mind and the center of mental activity. Therefore *xin* is nowadays usually translated into English as "heart-mind." The ambiguity—from a Western "logocentristic" perspective—indicates that early philosophy in general, and Daoism in particular, did not engage in a specific "philosophy of mind" and that the mind as such was hardly ever a philosophical topic. In Daoism, the "mind" is more or less understood in bodily terms. It is integrated into the functioning of the body and is not a separate force or constructive power. I believe that this constitutes one of the main differences between early Daoist philosophy and later Chan Buddhism: When early Daoists referred to *xin*, they were dealing with the heart-mind, while later Chan Buddhists were referring with the same term to Buddhist notions of consciousness.

Another philosophical difference between Chan and Daoism, as I see it, regards the assessment of the "reality of the real." Daoist philosophy, as I hoped to show, generally affirms the world of "presence" (*you*), that is, all the "ten thousand things," life and death, even action and speech. The nonpresence (*wu*) in the midst of presence—the emptiness that is neither dead nor alive and neither acts nor speaks—does not expose any "relativity" of the present. Daoist emptiness and nonpresence do not diminish but rather confirm the authenticity of the present.

In comparison with Daoism, Chan has a more ambiguous concept of the reality of the real. Like Daoism, Chan also affirms the authenticity of the here and now, but it also affirms its inauthenticity. The Chan Buddhist ambivalence in regard to the reality of the real is evident in its well-known "rule of three": A mountain is a mountain. A mountain is not a mountain. A mountain is a mountain. The first statement represents the immediate affirmation of the real as real by the "prephilosophical" consciousness. In the course of Chan Buddhist practice, the reality of the real is paradoxically challenged by the mind. This is expressed with the statement that says that a mountain is not a mountain. Finally, when enlightenment is attained, even the paradoxical challenge of the authenticity of the real is acknowledged as being authentic and is thus integrated into the state of authentic existence. In the end, the inauthentic is also accepted as authentic, and this is represented by the final statement that again sees the mountain as a mountain. This third level of reality is not to be equated with the first; it is more complex and has integrated or "superseded" its own negation.

While Daoist emptiness and nonpresence contribute to the genuineness of the reality of the real, Chan Buddhism indeed ends up with some sort of "relativism." For Chan Buddhists, the real is always in a dialectical relation with the unreal. There is a constant dialectical tension between the real and the unreal that constitutes reality. A good illustration of this attitude and "the combination of Daoism and Buddhism" is the following text by the Daoist Tan Qiao who lived in the tenth century CE. This text reflects the Chan Buddhist turn of later Daoism. It is taken from Tan Qiao's "Book of Alternations" (*Huashu*) and describes a Daoist-Chan-Buddhist room of mirrors in which the images in the mirror are again infinitely mirrored in opposite mirrors:

A mirror reflects the shape, another mirror reflects the image. Mirror and mirror reflect each other. Image and image transmit each other without altering the shape of the [mirrored] sword, and without taking away the color of the [mirrored] robe. It is the same shape which is not different from the image, and it is the same image which is not different from the shape. Thus one realizes the shape as not real and the image as not unreal. Not real and not unreal—this is in accord with the Dao.[3]

Tan Qiao's image of the room of mirrors is obviously indebted to an earlier Buddhist example. It is said that Fazang (643–712), the great master of Chinese Huayan Buddhism, once used a similar installation—a room of mirroring mirrors with an illuminated statue of the Buddha in the middle—to introduce the Empress Wu to the mysteries of the Buddhist teachings.[4] Fazang's illuminated Buddha statue, as well as Tan Qiao's sword and robe, are supposed to demonstrate how the real and the unreal interpenetrate and depend on each other. The real and the unreal are in a relation of relativity. Therefore, the unreal is no less real than the real; and the real is no less unreal than the unreal. Such a dialectics of reality and appearance is introduced into Daoist philosophy only through contact with Buddhism. Ancient pre-Buddhist Daoism affirms the full reality of the real. The allegory of Duke Niuai and his "illness of change" showed unmistakably that even in the process of ongoing change, the segments of change lose nothing of their authenticity.[5]

Another difference, more institutional than doctrinal, between Daoism and Chan is the more religious character of the latter. Neither Laozi nor Zhuangzi are portrayed in the ancient texts as "priests" in a religious community. Even though both Laozi and Zhuangzi are portrayed as masters who answer the questions of disciples, the sources do not indicate that they were revered as religious leaders by "monks." Even though Chan Buddhists were extremely critical of Buddhist religious institutions, many of them lived in monasteries. Before Daoist religion developed, Laozi and Zhuangzi were usually portrayed as individual teachers without a specific group of followers. Laozi was traditionally believed to have left the country completely on his own—and to have sometimes disputed with Confucius—while Zhuangzi typically appears in discussion with philosophical opponents such as Hui Shi.

The more religious character of Chan Buddhism is also demonstrated by the nature of its most important writings. The *Laozi* is a collection of philosophical poetry, and the *Zhuangzi* is a book that includes allegories, dialogues, and short philosophical treatises. In contrast, Chan Buddhist scriptures are often sermonlike speeches (like the famous "Sutra of the Sixth Patriarch") or records of the sayings and deeds of important priests (the so-called *yulu*) as noted down by the monks in the monasteries.

2. Daoism and Contemporary Philosophy

Having reviewed the ancient Chinese philosophy of Daoism, the legitimate question may arise: Is Daoism still relevant? What, if anything, can Daoism contribute to present-day thought? What are we to do with Daoism? Is it just an exotic teaching of long gone times from a faraway land, or is there something about it that has an actual interest for today?

I believe that Daoism is still relevant today, maybe even astonishingly relevant—and its relevance may indeed be very philosophical. It may help in overcoming some outdated patterns of "Western" thought that do not correspond to a "postmodern" world. Many contemporary philosophers *no longer* believe in the validity of various traditional "Western" philosophical concepts. Daoism, on the other hand, did *not yet* believe in these concepts. There may well be some surprising coincidences between the present *no longer* and the ancient *not yet*. In the remaining pages, I will try to explore some.

A core element of Daoist philosophy is the affirmation of the full authenticity of all there is. Critics of the Western philosophical tradition have often pointed out a certain lack of affirmation, particular in the Platonic-Christian tradition. One of the most fervent critics of Western philosophy and its specific lack of affirmation, or its "nihilism," was Friedrich Nietzsche—who may also rightfully be called a "grandfather" of postmodernism. Nietzsche tried to find a "new way towards the yes," and Daoism may assist post-Nietzscheans in moving this way. Nietzsche explains in regard to the new way towards the yes that it may lead to "a Dionysian yes-saying to the world as it is, including the wish of its absolute return and eternity—with which there would be a new ideal of philosophy and sensibility." [6]

Nietzsche's affirmation—like the Daoist one—is the result of a negation, a negation of one's old identity, a negation of one's "individuality." This negation enables one to take on the zero-perspective and leads to an unrestricted affirmation of the "world as it is." Unlike Daoism, Nietzsche, of course, had an overcoming of both the Christian "pessimism" and "individual" in mind, though in his attempt he still keeps its vocabulary when he talks of "eternity." However, Nietzsche's eternity seems to be quite distinct from the old Christian "transcendent" eternity. His affirmation of an "eternal return" is an affirmation of the immanence of all there is; it is a "new sensibility" for the purpose-free unfolding of life, for the becoming and the passing of life, for the "Dionysian world of an eternal-self-creation and an eternal-self-destruction."[7]

The Nietzschean affirmation of life and death resembles the Daoist affirmation of these two phases, and in both cases goes along with a criticism of "nihilistic" morality. When Nietzsche—as quoted above—wrote about his new way towards the yes and a new philosophical sensibility, he also talked about a new "amorality" that went along with it. Nietzsche, the first philosophical psychoanalyst of Western morality, tried to find a way out of the Christian traditional semantics of *sin*. Like the Daoists, who tried to find a way out of the Confucian semantics of *shame*, Nietzsche also tried to eliminate the moral overburdening of the ego by eliminating the ego itself.

Nietzsche and Daoism represent two kinds of "fundamental innocentisms," to use an expression coined by the contemporary German philosopher Peter Sloterdijk. Both Nietzsche and Daoism saw the dominating moral discourses of their time—the Christian and the Confucian ones—as "nihilist" obstructions of the affirmative attitude toward the process of life and birth, of becoming and passing. To them, these traditional moralities imposed a good/bad or a good/evil pattern on all that happens, and thus covered up the actual complexity and even the actual aesthetics of the world. The moral perspective makes it hard to accept the genuineness of the world as it is, and it leads to aesthetic and theoretical stiffness, to an insensitivity towards the unfolding of events. The Daoists tried to preserve this openness to the world, and thus they looked upon fixed moral perspectives and distinctions with great suspicion. In the *Zhuangzi*, there appears a legendary Daoist sage named Xu You who conceives of morality as something pathological. When this Daoist sage was approached by a person who had just been visiting the Confucian model of morality, the sage ruler Yao, the following dialogue arises:

> Xu You [the Daoist master] said [to Yi Erzi, the man approaching him]: "What kind of assistance has Yao [the Confucian sage and model of morality] been giving you?"
> Yi Erzi said: "Yao told me: 'You must learn to practice benevolence and righteousness and to speak clearly about right and wrong.'"
> "Then why come to see me?" said Xu You. "Yao has already tattooed you with benevolence and righteousness and cut off your nose with right and wrong. Now how do you expect to go wandering in any far-away, carefree, and as-you-like-it paths?"
> "That may be," said Yi Erzi. "But I would like, if I may, to wander in a little corner of them."
> "Impossible!" said Xu You. "Eyes that are blind have no way to tell the loveliness of faces and features, eyes with no pupils have no way to tell the beauty of colored and embroidered silks."[8]

The Daoist master clearly regards the instruction of somebody who has been "infected" with Confucian morality as hopeless. He compares the exposure to morality with bodily mutilation inflicted by ancient Chinese legal punishment: the tattooing of the skin and the cutting off of the nose. From a Daoist point of view, such "mutilation" prevents people from taking the course of the Daoist way, the so-called "wandering in any far-away, carefree, and as-you like it paths." Looking at the world through the eyes of morality and applying the distinction of right and wrong is compared to be being blind or having eyes without pupils that are unable "to tell the loveliness of faces and features" and "the beauty of colored and embroidered silks." Once harmed by the moral outlook, one has become truly—in the literal sense of the word *in-sane.*

Oddly enough, these characteristics of the ancient Daoist critique of morality—the imagery of pathology, the conception of moral distinctions as something superimposed on more basic distinctions, and the conception of ethics as a critical reflection on and warning against morality—reappear, albeit within a totally different theoretical context, in an eminent German sociologist's analysis of its role in the present-day world. Thus, the Daoist dialogue quoted above may serve as a kind of premodern prelude to the "negative ethics" of postmodern times. Most likely totally unaware of his strange Daoist predecessors, Niklas Luhmann, the German "Anti-Habermas," if one might say so, declared: "In normal everyday interaction, after all, morality is not needed anyway; it is always a symptom of the occurrence of pathologies."[9] Luhmann's skepticism is grounded on the observation of a certain "problem of morality": "Whenever the catchword 'morality' appears, the experiences Europe has had with morality since the Middle Ages should actually demonstrate this problem well: religiously adorned upheavals and suppressions, the horrors of inquisition, wars all about morally binding truths and revolt arising in indignation."[10]

The current political and military situation in the world proves this statement to still be true. Daoism, just like modern and postmodern criticisms of morality, exposes the proximity of moral discourse and distinction to violent deeds. None of these criticisms of morality advocates immorality—but all of them argue for a certain skepticism in regard to heavily moral language and moral attitudes; they argue for a certain dose of intellectual amorality.

By avoiding any fixation of the ego or adoption of a moral perspective and also by affirming the equal authenticity of life and death, Daoism took a different path than the Platonic-Christian tradition and its "humanism." The nondevelopment of a strong notion of subjectivity in Daoism prevented the development of a specifically human "soul," of the human being as an image of a transcendent God, and of humanity as the "crown of creation." The Western humanist tradition conceived of the world as basically the world of man, as an environment built around and for humans. Daoism, on the other hand, never took humans nearly as seriously. When Daoist texts explain the Dao, they refer to examples such as the wheel or the root, they talk about the happiness of fish and about people changing into butterflies and tigers. It is maybe the parable of Hundun, the "emperor of the center,"[11] that demonstrates most drastically the Daoist skepticism about humanity. Once the "kind" kings of the periphery visit Hundun and drill seven holes into his body in order to supply him with a *human* face, Hundun dies. The kings of the periphery are very "humane"—and they want to "humanize" Hundun. But it is their humanity and their attempt to humanize the world that destroys him. Their actions are destructive to the "natural" order. The

Daoist criticism of moral humanity leads to a criticism of a too-humanist outlook on the world as such. A quite similar line of argumentation can be found in Nietzsche's philosophy. Nietzsche's criticism of Christian morality lead him to a criticism of the humanist tradition. The Nietzschean "overman" is not at all an Arian "superman" (as the Nazis would have liked to have it); he is rather a poetic symbol for the overcoming of the human, or all-to-human, perspective. The overman is not the "better man," he is rather a man who no longer limits himself to the narrow pattern of humanity. Nietzsche writes—and this reminds one very much of the old Hundun:

> *Main thought!* Not nature deceives us, the individuals, and promotes its ends by hoodwinking us: instead, the individuals arrange all Being according to individual—i.e. false—measures; we want to be right in this case, and consequently "nature" has to appear as a liar. In truth, there are no *individual truths*, instead there are merely individual *errors*. The *individual* itself is an *error*. Everything happening within us is in itself *something else* that we do not know: only we put the intention, the hoodwinking and the morality into nature. – But I distinguish: the conceived-conceited individuals and the true "life-systems," which everyone among us is one—both are conflated into one, while "the individual" is only a sum of conscious feelings and judgments and errors, a *belief*, a little piece of the true life-system, or many little pieces, thought and imagined to be unified, a "unit" that does not hold. We are buds on One tree—what do we know about what may become of us in the interest of that tree! But we have a consciousness, as if we would want to and should be *Everything*, a fantasy of "I" and all "Non-I." *Ceasing to feel being such a fantastical ego! Learning step by step to throw off the supposed individual!* Discovering the errors of the ego! Looking into egotism as an error! Don't you ever conceive of its opposite as altruism! This would be the love of the *other supposed* individuals! No! **Beyond** "me" and "you"! **Feeling cosmic.**[12]

The ancient Daoist and the new Nietzschean nonhumanist but "cosmic" sensibility[13] does not have to result in a "new age" style natural religion—it may rather result in a new approach to the development of a theory for the postmodern world. The contemporary German philosophers Peter Sloterdijk (who wrote a book called *Euro-Daoism*)[14] and Niklas Luhmann are two thinkers who have suggested a nonhumanist interpretation of the functioning of present-day society. In one of his articles, Sloterdijk says: "By the establishment of mass culture through the media in the First World after 1918 (radio) and after 1945 (TV), and even more by the current internet revolutions the coexistence of men in present-day society has been put on new foundations. These are, as it can be shown without difficulties, distinctly post-literary, post-epistolographic, and consequently post-humanist."[15]

Sloterdijk adds to this analysis the following diagnosis: "The era of modern Humanism as a model for education and culture has come to an end because the illusion that the large-scale political and economic structures can still be organized according to the beloved model of a literary society is no longer tenable."[16] Humanist theories—including modernized versions such as that of Juergen Habermas—are unable to offer credible descriptions of the new social functioning of the era of globalization. Many people may find this, as Sloterdijk seems to indicate, worrisome and regrettable, but such regrets are to no theoretical and philosophical avail.

Our world has ceased to be ours, and it does not help if we try to supply it with a hand-made human face. The functioning of the modern economy has to be explained largely in terms of the flow of money and stocks—and no longer as a causal result of human enterprise. The global exercise of political power and its distribution can no longer be sufficiently analyzed by attributing it to individual humans and their private decisions. Likewise, mass communication has quite obviously detached itself from actual human performances and "autonomized" itself as a self-generating "hypertext." In the face of these developments, a "systemic turn" has taken place in social theory. Theoreticians like Niklas Luhmann try to overcome the assumption that "society consists of concrete human beings and of relationships between them" and that "consequently a society constitutes or integrates itself by consensus between human beings, by congruency of their opinions and complementarities of their ends."[17] Instead, it is suggested, society constructs itself through communication, similar, for instance, to a biological organism that constructs itself through its own physiological operations. Society is described as a self-generating or *autopoietic* evolutionary process, but one without a pre-established evolutionary direction. Systems theory tries to remove the artificial human features that are drilled into social functioning by customary semantics.

Contemporary thinkers like Sloterdijk and Luhmann try to describe society as an *autopoietic* process, and this connects—albeit on a much more elaborate theoretical level—to Nietzsche's vision of a "Dionysian world of an eternal-self-creation and an eternal-self-destruction." Interestingly enough, it also connects—although much less immediately—to an ancient Daoist philosophy of a nonteleological, continuous sequence of becoming and passing away.

New theoreticians of society follow in Nietzsche's footsteps when they leave the trodden path of humanism, individualism, and morality behind. But as posthumanists, postindividualists, and postmoralists, these thinkers also share some common ground with a prehumanist, preindividualistic, and premoralistic philosophy such as ancient Daoism. It may sound farfetched to say that new "postmodern" theories are closer to ancient Chinese thought than they are to ancient Greek philosophy—but these contemporary theories explicitly aim at overcoming the "old-European" tradition, and so find themselves in an unexpected proximity to philosophies that were never a part of this tradition. If there is any philosophical future for Daoist thought, I believe that it lies in what it can contribute to a new understanding of contemporary society beyond the rhetorics of morality and humanism.

Notes

PREFACE AND INTRODUCTION

1. Roger T. Ames and David Hall, *Daodejing: "Making This Life Significant"; A Philosophical Translation* (New York: Ballantine, 2003); Robert G. Henricks, trans., Lao-Tzu, *Te-Tao Ching* (New York: Ballantine, 1989) and *Lao-Tzu's Tao Te Ching* (New York: Columbia University Press, 2000); Philip J. Ivanhoe, trans., *The Daodejing of Laozi* (Indianapolis and Cambridge: Hackett, 2002).

2. See the English translation: William H. Nienhauser, ed., *The Grand Scribe's Records* (Bloomington, Indiana: Indiana University Press, 1994), 21–23.

3. On Legalism and Hanfeizi, see part II, 1 below.

4. In *The Grand Scribe's Records*, this information on Zhuangzi directly follows the information on Laozi. See note 2 above.

5. *Dahui Pujue chanshi yulu*. In *Taisho shinshu daizokyo*, vol. 47, chap. 22 (Tokyo, 1924–1932), 904a. All translations are mine if not otherwise indicated.

6. An English edition of the text by Leo S. Chang and Yu Feng translates the title less literally but in accordance with its content: *The Four Political Treatises of the Yellow Emperor* (Honolulu: University of Hawai'i Press, 1998).

7. This text is believed to be a compilation of materials dating back to the third century BCE.

8. This text is from the second century BCE.

9. The expression "ten thousand [kinds of] things" (*wan wu*) is a common Chinese term for "everything."

10. See part III, 1 below.

11. *Zhuangzi jishi*, in *Zhuzi jicheng* (Beijing: Zhonghua, 1954), 52. See part I, 2 on Guo Xiang's philosophy.

12. Cf. the English translation by Richard B. Mather, *Shi-shuo Hsin yü: A New Account of Tales of the World* (Minneapolis: University of Minnesota Press, 1976).

13. See part III, 2 below.

14. Some scholars, especially in recent times, criticize the traditional distinction between (a more theoretical) Daoist philosophy (*dao jia*) and (a more practical) "Daoist religion" (*dao jiao*). (See, for instance, Livia Kohn, *Daoism and Chinese Culture* [Cambridge, MA: Three Pines Press, 2001], 1–7.) These scholars often correctly point out that such a distinction is historically problematic because even the early "philosophical" texts of Daoism indicate the existence of a "religious" practice, and the later Daoist practice was always closely related to "theoretical" texts. There are many excellent studies on Daoist practice available

in English. Since I do not systemically address these issues in the present book, I would like to refer the interested reader to the books by Livia Kohn, especially to her *Daoism Handbook* (Leiden: Brill, 2000); to Isabelle Robinet's *Taoism: Growth of a Religion*, trans. Phyllis Brooks (Stanford: Stanford University Press, 1997); and to James Miller's *Daoism: A Short Introduction* (Oxford: Oneworld Publications, 2003).

15. For details see Kohn, *Daoism Handbook*.

16. Another, less documented, early Daoist community was named the Taiping or "Great Peace." See Kohn, *Daoism and Chinese Culture*, 67–68.

17. See Kohn, *Daoism and Chinese Culture*, 68–71.

18. Two of the six books are translated into English: *The Spirit of Chinese Philosophy*, trans. E. R. Hughes (London: Kegan Paul, 1947); and *A New Treatise on the Methodology of Metaphysics*, trans. C. I. Wang (Beijing: Foreign Languages Press, 1997). I have published a German translation of this book in my study *Die philosophischste Philosophie: Feng Youlans Neue Metaphysik* (Wiesbaden: Harrassowitz, 2000).

19. Feng Youlan, "Chinese Philosophy and a Future World Philosophy," *The Philosophical Review* 57 (1948): 540.

20. Ibid., 543.

21. I am introducing here the expression the "self-overcoming of rationalism" in analogy to Graham Parkes's expression the "self-overcoming of nihilsm" in regard to the Kyoto School philosopher Nishitani Keiji. (See Nishitani Keiji, *The Self-Overcoming of Nihilism*, trans. Graham Parkes and Setsuko Aihara [Albany: SUNY Press, 1990.]) Although Feng and Nishitani (or, on a larger scale, New Confucianism and the Kyoto School) connect to different "trends" in Western philosophy, they deal with them in an astonishingly similar manner. Both try to show that by means of an Eastern "mysticism," the deficits of these Western approaches can be exposed and finally amended by way of a "self-overcoming."

22. Feng, "Chinese Philosophy and a Future World Philosophy," 543.

23. Ibid., 544.

24. Ibid., 545.

25. Shanghai: Commercial Press, 1946, 97. Cf. the English translation by C. I. Wang (see note 18 above), p. 114.

26. The translator was Zhang Songnian. The translation appeared in the leading Chinese philosophical journal *Zhexue pinglun* 1 (1927–1928): 5, 6.

27. In his autobiography, Feng writes: "Another pressing reason for writing this book (i.e.: the *New Methodology*) was to explain the difference between (my own) New Metaphysics and the Vienna School. I recalled meeting Wittgenstein in 1933, when I went to England to give lectures at Oxford. He invited me to his rooms for tea, and I found there was quite an affinity in our views. We did not talk on any specialized subjects, but we had a congenial conversation. I could tell that he, too, was interested in the problem of the inconceivable and the unspeakable. However, the Vienna School viewed philosophy as a matter of linguistic or scientific methodology, whereas I thought philosophy had something to say in its own right. In hopes of explaining this view, I put a few things in writing." From Feng Youlan, *The Hall of Three Pines: An Account of My Life*, trans. Denis C. Mair (Honolulu: University of Hawaii Press, 2000), 279. (Translation modified.)

28. It is somewhat astonishing that more recent research in affinities between Wittgenstein and Chinese philosophy tends to ignore Feng's important and immediate relation to him.

29. See Reinhard May, *Heidegger's Hidden Sources: East-Asian Influences on His Work*, trans. Graham Parkes (London: Routledge, 1996). See also the special issue on Heidegger and Daoism of the *Journal of Chinese Philosophy* 30/1 (2003), especially Wing-Cheuk Chan's article "Phenomenology of Technology: East and West" (1–18) and Guenter Wohlfart's article "Heidegger and Laozi: *Wu* (Nothing)—on Chapter 11 of the *Dao De Jing*" (39–60).

30. In *Der Ursprung des Kunstwerks, Feldweg-Gespräche*, and *Das Ding*.

31. See Paul Shih-yi Hsiao, "Heidegger and Our Translation of the Tao Te Ching," in *Heidegger and Asian Thought*, ed. Graham Parkes (Honolulu: University of Hawai'i Press, 1987).

32. He does so, for instance, in *Unterwegs zur Sprache, Überlieferte Sprache und technische Sprache, Grundsätze des Denkens*, and *Wissenschaft und Besinnung*.

33. For Heidegger's reception of the *Zhuangzi*, see Graham Parkes, "Thoughts on the Way: *Being and Time* via Lao-Chuang," in *Heidegger and Asian Thought*, ed. Graham Parkes, 105–144.

34. Mihaly Csikszsentmihaly, *Flow: The Psychology of Optimal Experience* (New York: Harper Collins, 1990). Interestingly enough, Csikszsentmihaly himself illustrates his concept with examples from the *Zhuangzi*. On the flow experience and Daoist philosophy, see the interesting article by Chris Jochim, "Just Say No to 'No Self' in *Zhuangzi*," in *Wandering at Ease in the Zhuangzi*, ed. Roger T. Ames (Albany: State University of New York Press, 1998), 35–74.

35. On "sitting in forgetfulness" see *Zhuangzi yinde* (Beijing, 1946), 19/6/92, and *Chuang-Tzu: The Inner Chapters*, trans. A. C. Graham (Indianapolis and Cambridge: Hackett, 2001), 92. On the "losing of the 'I'" see the discussion of the allegory of the "pipe of heaven" in part III, 1 below.

PART I
IMAGES AND ALLEGORIES

1. Robinet, *Taoism: Growth of a Religion*, 14.

2. *Guanzi*, in *Zhuzi jicheng* (Beijing: Zhonghua, 1954), 220. See also part II, 2 below.

3. This story concludes the seventh and last of the Inner Chapters of the *Zhuangzi*. The text says: "The Emperor of the South Sea was Fast, the Emperor of the North Sea was Furious, the Emperor of the center was Hundun. At one time, Fast and Furious met in the land of Hundun, who treated them very generously. Fast and Furious then discussed how to repay Hundun's bounty. 'All men have seven holes through which they look, listen, eat, breathe; he alone doesn't have any. Let's try boring them.' Every day they bored one hole, and on the seventh day Hundun died" (*Chuang-Tzu: The Inner Chapters*, trans. A. C. Graham, 98. Translation modified).

4. *Zhuangzi jishi*, in *Zhuzi jicheng*, 139.

5. See Sarah Allan, *The Way of Water and Sprouts of Virtue* (Albany: State University of New York Press, 1997).

6. The symbolics of water is also connected with the many Daoist allegories about *swimming*. See parts I, 2, p. 62–65 and II, 6 below.

7. See chapter 6 of the *Daodejing* as discussed in the following section for a combination of the images of the valley, the gate, and the female.

8. See the section "Daoist Mysticism" in the introduction above.

9. David Hall and Roger T. Ames have introduced this neologism. They say, "The classical Chinese are primarily acosmotic thinkers. By 'acosmotic' we shall mean that they do not depend in the majority of their speculations upon either the notion that the totality of things (*wan wu* or *wan you*, the 'ten thousand things') has a radical beginning, or that these things constitute a single-ordered world." In *Anticipating China: Thinking through the Narratives of Chinese and Western Culture* (Albany: State University of New York Press, 1995), 184. The usage of the world "radical" is a bit unfortunate in the definition since it literally means "rooted"—while Hall and Ames seem to understand "radical" here in the sense of "absolute." The "acosmotic" worldview, in a way, believes in a "radical" beginning, but not as an "absolute" beginning. The Daoist beginning is truly "radical" since it is an integral part of that which is.

10. *Chuang Tzu: Taoist Philosopher and Chinese Mystic*, trans. Herbert A. Giles, 2nd rev. ed. (London: Allen and Unwin, 1926), 47. Transcription modified. Giles's translation was first published in 1889.

11. A very good study on this issue is Donald Phillip Verene, *Hegel's Recollection: A Study of Images in the Phenomenology of Spirit* (Albany: State University of New York Press, 1985).

12. A more literal translation is, "The not-knowing about a butterfly at this moment is not different from the not-knowing about a Zhuang Zhou during the time of the dream." *Zhuangzi jishi*, in *Zhuzi jicheng*, 54.

13. Ibid., 53–54.

14. Ibid., 54.

15. *Huainanzi*, in *Zhuzi jicheng* (Beijing: Zhonghua, 1954), 20–21.

16. *Zi* means "Master" and was a common "title" for philosophers in China; examples are Lao-zi (Master Lao), Kong-zi, (Master Kong, or "Confucius"), Meng-zi (Master Meng or "Mencius").

17. In Chinese, the family name precedes the personal name. Zhuang is a family name, and Zhou is a personal name.

18. *Zhuangzi yinde*, 4/2/30. See *Chuang-Tzu: The Inner Chapters*, trans. A. C. Graham, 53. When I cite both Chinese- and English-language sources for a primary text in my notes, this indicates that the quotation substantially follows the English-language source, but that I have occasionally changed the wording.

19. *The Complete Works of Chuang Tzu*, trans. Burton Watson (New York and London: Columbia University Press, 1968). For the Chinese text, see *Zhuangzi yinde*, 75/26/48–49.

20. See part III, 2 below.

21. See my article "Zhuangzi's Fishnet Allegory: A Text-Critical Analysis," *Journal of Chinese Philosophy* 27:4 (2000), 489–502, for an analysis of Wang Bi's

reading of the fishnet allegory.

22. R. H. Mathews, *A Chinese-English Dictionary Compiled for the China Inland Mission* (Shanghai: China Inland Mission and Presbyterian Mission Press, 1931), 6161.41.

23. Ibid., 6161.43.

24. *Zhuangzi yinde*, 7/28/7. Here the text says: "Wandering carefree between heaven and earth—and the heart is satisfied by itself" (*xin yi zi de*).

25. For a discussion of philological evidence from other Daoist texts—namely from the *Liezi* and the commentary to this text by Zhang Zhan (fourth century CE)—for this paradoxical usage of the phrase *de yi*, see my article "Zhuangzi's Fishnet Allegory: A Text-Critical Analysis," 496.

26. *Zhuangzi yinde*, 43/17/24. *Zhuangzi jishi*, in *Zhuzi jicheng*, 253.

27. *Zhuangzi yinde*, 52/21/4.

28. Ibid., 64/23/48.

29. Ibid., 61/24/96.

30. The *Liezi* is a compilation of mainly Daoist materials put together in the third or fourth century CE. It thus goes back to the same age as Guo Xiang's edition of the present-day *Zhuangzi*.

31. *Liezi*, in *Zhuzi jicheng* (Beijing: Zhonghua, 1954), 43.

32. *Zhuangzi jishi*, in *Zhuzi jicheng*, 407.

33. Yang Wanli, *Chengzhai ji*, in *Sibu Congkan* 1 (Shanghai, 1919–1936), chap. 83, 690a–b.

34. A. C. Graham, trans., *Chuang-Tzu: The Inner Chapters*, 123. (Translation modified.) See also *Zhuangzi yinde*, 45/17/87–92.

35. *Zhuangzi jishi*, in *Zhuzi jicheng*, 268.

36. The *Zhuangzi*, however, contains the story of such a "miracle." See part II, 6 below.

37. *Zhuangzi yinde*, 46/18/11.

PART II
ISSUES

1. A. C. Graham, trans., *Chuang-Tzu: The Inner Chapters*, 122–23. (Translation modified.) *Zhuangzi yinde*, 45/17/84–87.

2. *Zhuangzi yinde*, 34/13/18–21.

3. Burton Watson, trans., *Han Fei Tzu: Basic Writings* (New York, London: Columbia University Press, 1964), 32. See *Hanfeizi*, in *Zhuzi jicheng* (Beijing: Zhonghua, 1954), 28.

4. Marcel Granet, *Chinese Civilization*, trans. Kathleen E. Innes and Mabel R. Brailsford (London: Routledge & Kegan Paul, 1930), 208.

5. *Guanzi*, in *Zhuzi jicheng*, 220. See W. Allyn Rickett, trans., *Guanzi: Political, Economic and Philosophical Essays from Early China* (Princeton: Princeton University Press, 1998), 75. (Translation modified.)

6. The original French version was published in 1982 in Paris. An English translation was published in 1993 in Berkeley by University of California Press.

7. See part I, 1, "The Wheel—an Image of the Dao," above.

8. Ryan O'Neill indicated to me a saying of the Presocratic philosopher Anaximander that seems to parallel this Daoist concept. Anaximander's testimonia 12A9 (Diels/Kranz) says: "Whence things have their origin, there they must also pass away according to necessity; for they must pay penalty and be judged for their injustice, according to the ordinance of time."

9. See the following quotation and the allegory of the flute discussed in part III, 1 below.

10. *Zhuangzi yinde*, 63/23/42.

11. See the allegory of the flute discussed in part III, 1 below.

12. Kristofer Schipper, *The Taoist Body* (Berkeley: University of California Press, 1993), 108, 235.

13. Wolfgang Bauer, "Das Stirnrunzeln des Totenkopfs. Über die Paradoxie des Todes in der frühen chinesischen Philosophie," in *Der Tod in den Weltkulturen und Weltreligionen*, ed. C. von Barlowen (Munich: Diederichs, 1996), 261.

14. *Zhuangzi yinde*, 60/22/74; *Zhuangzi jishi*, in *Zhuzi jicheng*, 332.

15. See part I, 2, "The Dream of the Butterfly—Or: Everything Is Real" above.

16. *Zhuangzi yinde*, 6/2/78–82; *Zuangzi jishi*, in *Zhuzi jicheng*, 49–50. See A. C. Graham, trans., *Chuang-Tzu: The Inner Chapters*, 59–60.

17. See *Zhuangzi yinde*, 15/7/7-8.

18. Ibid., 6/2/73. See A. C. Graham, trans., *Chuang-Tzu: The Inner Chapters*, 58.

19. *Zhuangzi yinde*, 17/6/41 See A. C. Graham, trans., *Chuang-Tzu: The Inner Chapters*, 87.

20. *Zhuangzi yinde*, 52/20/21.

21. *Zhuangzi yinde*, 18/6/75–82. *Zhuangzi jishi*, in *Zhuzi jicheng*, 124–26. See A. C. Graham, trans., *Chuang-Tzu: The Inner Chapters*, 90–91.

22. *Zhuangzi yinde*, 17/6/46. See A. C. Graham, trans., *Chuang-Tzu: The Inner Chapters*, 87.

23. *Zhuangzi yinde*, 60/22/77.

24. The German verb *aufheben* has the three meanings: a) to preserve, to keep; b) to lift, to raise; c) to abolish, to annul.

25. *Zhuangzi yinde*, 70/25/15. *Zhuangzi jishi*, in *Zhuzi jicheng*, 382. See A. C. Graham, trans., *Chuang-Tzu: The Inner Chapters*, 110.

26. *Zhuangzi jishi*, in *Zhuzi jicheng*, 382.

27. *Zhuangzi yinde*, 42/17/15–19. See A. C. Graham, trans., *Chuang-Tzu: The Inner Chapters*, 145–46.

28. *Zhuangzi yinde*, 5/2/49, *Zhuangzi jishi*, in *Zhuzi jicheng*, 38. See A. C. Graham, trans., *Chuang-Tzu: The Inner Chapters*, 55.

29. See section "Daoism Today" in the introduction above.

30. Marcel Granet, *La pensée chinoise* (Paris: Editions Albin Michel, 1934), 268. (My translation.)

31. Ibid., 267–68. (My translation.)

32. On the symbolics of the shadow in ancient China, see Rolf Trauzettel, "Der Schatten in chinesischer Kunst, Literatur und Philosophie: Leeres Zeichen und Zeichen der Leere," *Zeitschrift für Semiotik* 22 (2/2000): 183–208.

33. *Zhuangzi yinde*, 4/2/29–31. See A. C. Graham, trans., *Chuang-Tzu: The Inner Chapters*, 52–53.

34. Granet, *La pensée chinoise*, 108.

35. See Chen Guying, *Yi zhuan yu daojia sixiang* [The *Great Commentary* and Daoist Thought] (Beijing: Sanlian shudian, 1997).

36. *Dazhuan* (or: *Xici*), chapt. 2.

37. Granet, *La pensée chinoise*, 269. (My translation).

38. *Zhuangzi yinde*, 7/3/2–8/3/12. See A. C. Graham, trans., *Chuang-Tzu: The Inner Chapters*, 63–64.

39. *Zhuangzi yinde*, 50/19/49-54. See A. C. Graham, trans., *Chuang-Tzu: The Inner Chapters*, 136.

40. *Liezi*, in *Zhuzi jicheng*, 20. See A. C. Graham, trans., *The Book of Lieh-tzu* (New York: Columbia University Press, 1990), 44.

41. See *Liezi*, in *Zhuzi jicheng*, 20.

42. Ludwig Wittgenstein, *Philosophical Investigations*, 150.

43. *Zhuangzi yinde*, 50/19/54–58. See A. C. Graham, trans., *Chuang-Tzu: The Inner Chapters*, 135.

44. *Zhuangzi jishi*, in *Zhuzi jicheng*, 290.

45. On the history of this legend, see Shieh Jhy-Wey, "Grenze wegen Öffnung geschlossen. Zur Legende vom chinesischen maler, der in seinem Bild verschwindet," in *Zeichen lessen, Lese-zeichen: Kultursemiotische Vergleiche von Leseweisen in Deutschland und China*, ed. Jürgen Wertheimer and Susanne Göße (Tübingen: Stauffenburg, 1999), 201–26. The legend is also discussed in Roger Goepper, *Vom Wesen chinesischer Malerei* (Munich: Prestel, 1962). My account of the legend follows Goepper's summary on p. 26.

46. See Goepper, *Vom Wesen chinesischer Malerei*, 24.

47. *Mencius* 2A: 6.

48. Quoted from the translation by W. K. Liao, *The Complete Works of Han Fei Tzu: A Classic of Chinese Political Science*, vol. 1 (London: Arthur Probsthain, 1959), 214–15. See *Hanfeizi jijie*, in *Zhuzi jicheng* (Beijing, 1954), 118–19.

49. W. K. Liao remarks on page 215 that this "was the name of a star supposed to superintend the life-and-death problem of every mortal."

50. The important role of fear—not only fear of sickness—in Chinese cultural and social history may well be understood in connection with the Daoist insistence on prevention. On fear in Chinese culture, see a seminal article by Rolf Trauzettel: "Chinesische Reflexionen über Furcht und Angst: Ein Beitrag zur Mentalitätsgeschichte Chinas im Mittelalter und in der frühen Neuzeit," *Saeculum* 43.4 (1992): 307–24.

51. Robinet, *Taoism: Growth of a Religion*, 261.

52. See section on the fishnet allegory in part I, 2 above.

53. *Zhuangzi yinde*, 2/1/22. See A.C. Graham, trans., *Chuang-Tzu: The Inner Chapters*, 45.

54. *Zhuangzi yinde*, 72/25/63–64.

55. *Zhuangzi yinde*, 72–73/25/76–77.

56. The equal reality of a thing's name and shape can be directly related to the equal epistemological validity of hearing and seeing in ancient Chinese

philosophy. The latter has been excellently analyzed by Jane Geany in her important study *On the Epistemology of the Senses in Early Chinese Thought* (Honolulu: University of Hawai'i Press, 2002).

57. *Zhuangzi yinde*, 72/25/69–61.
58. *Zhuangzi yinde*, 72/25/73.
59. *Zhuangzi yinde*, 73/25/77.
60. *Zhuangzi yinde*, 6/2/67–70. See A. C. Graham, trans., *Chuang-Tzu: The Inner Chapters*, 58.
61. *Zhuangzi yinde*, 73/25/81.
62. *Zhuangzi yinde*, 4/2/29–31.
63. *Zhuangzi jishi*, in *Zhuzi jicheng*, 33.
64. See part II, 5 above.

PART III
STRUCTURES

1. Granet, *La pensée chinoise*, 232. (My translation.)
2. See part II, 5 above.
3. Granet, *La pensée chinoise*, 167. (My translation.)
4. Granet, *La pensée chinoise*, 232–33. (My translation.)
5. *Zhuangzi yinde*, 3/2/4–8. See A. C. Graham, trans., *Chuang-Tzu: The Inner Chapters*, 48–49.
6. *Zhuangzi yinde*, 3/2/8–9. See A. C. Graham, trans., *Chuang-Tzu: The Inner Chapters*, 49.
7. *Zhuangzi jishi*, in *Zhuzi jicheng*, 24.
8. *Zhuangzi jishi*, in *Zhuzi jicheng*, 332.
9. Aristotle, *De Interpretatione*, 16a. Quoted from the translation by J. L. Ackrill, in *The Complete Works of Aristotle: The Revised Oxford Translation*, ed. Jonathan Barnes, vol. 1 (Princeton: Princeton University Press, 1984), 25.
10. The version of Pliny's legend as well as the remarks on ancient Greek conceptions of art are taken from Hermann Ulrich Asemissen and Gunter Schweikhart, *Malerei als Thema der Malerei* (Berlin, 1994), 12.
11. Quoted after Hermann Ulrich Asemissen and Gunter Schweikhart, *Malerei als Thema der Malerei*, 14.
12. *Zhuangzi yinde*, 72–73/25/76–77. As quoted above, in part II, 8 (on language and thought). On the issue of Daoist and ancient Chinese conceptions of language, signs, and being, see my article "Chinese Language Philosophy and Correlativism," *Bulletin of the Museum of Far Eastern Antiquities* 72 (2000): 92–111.
13. See above, part II, 6 (on art and artisanship).
14. In this regard one should also be aware of the emblematic qualities of the Chinese script that surely contributed to a conception of language as a present reality. On this issue see Rolf Trauzettel, "Bild und Schrift. Oder: Auf welche Weise sind chinesische Schriftzeichen Embleme?" in *Zeichen-Kunst: Zeichen und*

Interpretation, ed. W. Stegmeier, vol. 5 (Frankfurt/Main: Suhrkamp, 1999), 130–63.

15. For a more detailed analysis of this issue see my article "Erinnern und Vergesen: Gegensätzliche Strukturen in Europa und China," *Saeculum* 2 (1999): 235–46.

16. Pseudo-Dionysius, *De divines nominibus*, 980A, quoted from the translation by Colm Luibheid, *Pseudo-Dionysius: The Complete Works* (New York and Mahwah, NJ: Paulist Press, 1987), 128.

17. Pseudo-Dionysius, *De divines nominibus*, 981A, quoted from the translation by Colm Luibheid, *Pseudo-Dionysius: The Complete Works*, 129.

18. Pseudo-Dionysius, *De divines nominibus*, 644 A. See the translation by Colm Luibheid, *Pseudo-Dionysius: The Complete Works*, 62. This image relates to the "divine persons" and had been used by the Neo-Platonic philosopher Proclus to illustrate the relation between forms and matter. See W. Tritsch, *Dionysius Areopagita: Mystische Theologie und andere Schriften* (Munich, 1956), 45.

19. Pseudo-Dionysius, *De divines nominibus*, 916A, quoted from the translation by Colm Luibheid, *Pseudo-Dionysius: The Complete Works*, 118.

20. This is an allusion to chapter 25 of the *Daodejing*.

21. This is another allusion to chapter 25 of the *Daodejing*.

22. A contemporary of He Yan.

23. This is another allusion to chapter 25 of the *Daodejing*.

24. Compare the *Analects* of Confucius, 8:19.

25. This text has been preserved as quoted in Zhang Zhan's commentary on the *Liezi*. See the *Liezi* edition in *Zhuzi jicheng* (Beijing, 1957), 41. My translation has profited from the English translation by Wing-tsit Chan in *A Source Book in Chinese Philosophy* (Princeton: Princeton University Press, 1969), 324–25.

26. *Zhuangzi yinde*, 73/25/80.

27. The comparison between a Daoist semiotics of presence and a traditional Western semiotics of representation may be extended to a comparison with postmodern Western semiotics. Postmodern philosophy (or, at least, many philosophers who are labeled postmodernists, such as Jacques Derrida) has strongly criticized the concept of presence. According to this semiotics, signs do not primarily designate something "really" real. While the old-European concept of representation is based on the tension between "true" presence and appearing representation, postmodernism tends to deny such an essential distinction.

There seems to be correspondences between postmodern Western semiotics and an ancient Daoist semiotics of presence. The ancient semiotics of presence did *not yet* acknowledge a realm of representation—it holds on to an affirmation of the present—whereas a postmodern semiotics of significance (as I would call it) *no longer* acknowledges representation. This semiotics of significance denies any "real" or essential reality in connection with signification. The following table illustrates how these three patterns may be compared (see my article "Before and After Representation" in *Semiotica* 143 [1/2003]: 69–77):

	present	re-presenting
pattern of presence (Daoism)	signified—signifier	
Pattern of representation (old-European)	signified-	-signifier
pattern of significance (postmodern)		signified—signifier

PART IV
PERSPECTIVES

1. Feng Youlan, *A Short History of Chinese Philosophy* (New York: Macmillan, 1958), 341.

2. See part II, 2 above.

3. Tan Qiao, *Huashu*, in *Zhengtong daozang* (Taibei, 1962), 1032, 724; chap. 1, 3a–b.

4. See Zan Ning, *Song gao seng zhuan*, vol. 1 (Beijing, 1987), 89–90.

5. See chapter I, 2, "The Dream of the Butterfly—Or: Everything Is Real," above.

6. Friedrich Nietzsche, posthumous fragment 10 (3) (autumn 1887) in *Kritische Studienausgabe*, ed. Giorgio Colli and Mazzino Montinari, vol. 9 (Munich: DTV, 1999), 455. (My translation.)

7. Friedrich Nietzsche, posthumous fragment 38 (12) (1885) in *Kritische Studienausgabe*, ed. Giorgio Colli and Mazzino Montinari, vol. 11 (Munich: DTV, 1999), 611. (My translation.)

8. Quoted from the translation by Burton Watson: *The Complete Works of Chuang Tzu*, 89. See *Zhuangzi yinde* (Beijing 1947), 18/6/82–19/6/86.

9. Niklas Luhmann, *The Reality of the Mass Media*, trans. Kathleen Cross (Stanford, CA: Stanford University Press, 2000), 79.

10. Niklas Luhmann, "Ethik als Reflexionstheorie der Moral," in *Gesellschaftsstruktur und Semantik*, vol. 3 (Frankfurt/Main: Suhrkamp, 1993), 370. (My translation.)

11. See part I, 1, "The Wheel—an Image of the Dao," above.

12. Friedrich Nietzsche, posthumous fragment 11 (7) (spring-fall 1881), in *Kritische Studienausgabe*, ed. Giorgio Colli and Mazzino Montinari, vol. 11, 442–43. (My translation.) See Günter Wohlfart, *Friedrich Nietzsche: Die nachgelassenen Fragmente; Eine Auswahl* (Stuttgart: Reclam, 1996), 298–99.

13. Graham Parkes's article "Nietzsche und Zhuangzi: Ein Zwischenspiel" (in *Komparative Philosophie*, ed. Rolf Elberfeld, Johann Kreuzer, John Minford, and Günter Wohlfart [Munich: Fink, 1998], 213–22) presents an interesting

observation regarding Zhuangzi's and Nietzsche's "nonhumanist" philosophies. Parkes points out how both philosophies make ample use of nonhuman imagery. See also Graham Parkes, *Composing the Soul: Reaches of Nietzsche's Philosophy* (Chicago: University of Chicago Press, 1994).

14. Peter Sloterdijk, *Eurotaoismus* (Frankfurt/Main: Suhrkamp, 1989).

15. Peter Sloterdijk, *Nicht Gerettet: Versuche nach Heidegger* (Frankfurt/Main: Suhrkamp, 2001), 306–7. (My translation.)

16. Peter Sloterdijk, *Nicht Gerettet: Versuche nach Heidegger*, 307. (My translation.)

17. Niklas Luhmann, *Die Gesellschaft der Gesellschaft* (Frankfurt/Main: Suhrkamp, 1997), 24–25. (My translation.)

Index